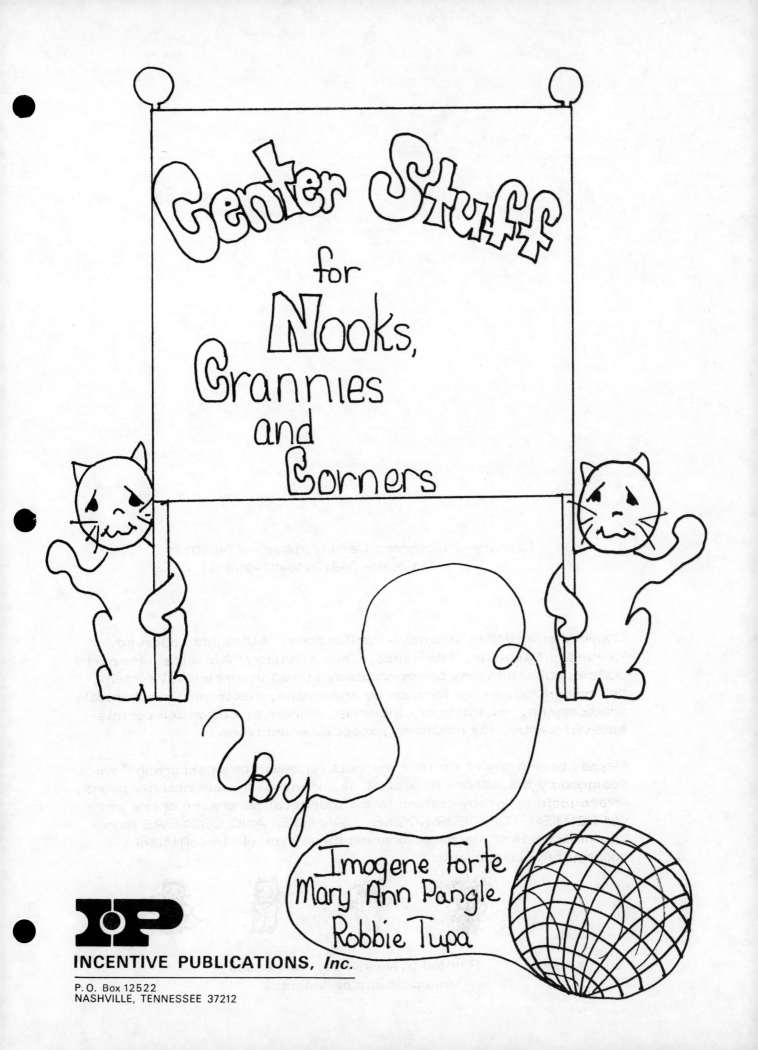

Center Stuff

for Nooks, Grannies and Corners

By

Imogene Forte
Mary Ann Pangle
Robbie Tupa

INCENTIVE PUBLICATIONS, Inc.

P.O. Box 12522
NASHVILLE, TENNESSEE 37212

Library of Congress Card Number – 77-670124
ISBN # – 0-913916-07-2

*

Printed in Nashville, Tennessee
United States of America

PREFACE

Center Stuff For Nooks Crannies and Corners
has been developed to help teachers use the
learning center approach to individualizing classroom instruction. Its conception is in direct
response to the many requests from readers of
Nooks, Crannies and Corners for a sequel teachers'
guidebook providing step-by-step directions for
planning and implementing a wide variety of classroom learning centers.

Each of the model learning centers presented contains performance
objectives, list of materials needed, procedures for implementation,
student activity sheets (with options), illustrations and an actual
photograph of the center in use. They are offered, not as the ultimate
in learning center design nor as the end to all ends in curriculum
planning. Instead it is hoped that they will help teachers and students
to become acclimated to the learning center concept and will provide
motivation for the production of original centers reflective of their
own interests and learning goals.

The centers have been kept as flexible and open-ended as possible.
They have been planned to be implemented in a variety of settings
to meet unique needs of a given group of students. Probably no two
teachers will use any model center in this book in exactly the same
way.

In rare instances the entire center plan may be adaptable to a classroom setting. Many times, however, it may be desirable to use
only a part or parts of a given center. Sometimes selected activities
may be combined with basal or other text related materials; teachers
will often find them to be companionable and supportive to directed
teaching sessions. At other times they may be used by individual
students on a contract or free choice basis. Even individual activities
within the centers have been structured to "stand alone" to give
teachers the widest possible range of choices in selection and
presentation. Hopefully, their actual implementation will be as
creative and as spontaneous as each teacher's imagination and
adaptation.

The cat symbols have been used to denote levels of difficulty
in presentation of content and skill development. Calling All
Cats is the basic knowledge level with intellectual and creative
expectancies ascending in this order: Cool Cat, Smarty Cat,
and finally Super Cat. As individual prescriptions are developed
to direct students to activities in the various centers, teachers
will want to exercise as much flexibility as possible to arrange
a center schedule that will be both challenging and satisfying to
each student. The activities are designed to be tailored to meet
individual needs, and are in no way dependent on ability grouping
or group scheduling.

The appendices have been included to provide reinforcement and
additional help to teachers who want to "open" their classrooms
for more creative learning.

We offer the complete centers, the games, the puzzles, the quizzes
and brain teasers, the other activity sheets, the additional ideas
and helpful hints and our very best wishes.

Imogene Forte
Mary Ann Pangle
Robbie Tupa

Nashville, Tennessee
November, 1973

With the exception of "Calling All Cats", all activity sheets
include student options.

TABLE OF CONTENTS

I. COMMUNICATIONS SKILLS DEVELOPMENT CENTERS

IV.   A VERY PRACTICAL APPENDIX

Communication Centers

·Notes·

ABC Order

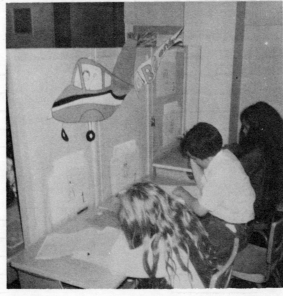

PURPOSE: After completing this center, the student should be able to arrange and use words in alphabetical order.

MATERIALS: Illustration and title
Tagboard
3-minute timer
Construction paper
Activity sheets
Clothesline, clothes pins
Small box

PROCEDURE:

1. Write each student's name on a 3" square of tagboard and put in a box, following directions given in "Super Cat" activity.

2. Place all materials in the center.

3. Introduce the center to enable the student to complete activities independently.

4. Provide time for evaluation of each completed activity and record individual student progress.

5. Make provision for filing or displaying completed activities.

3

ABC ORDER

Arrange each group of words in alphabetical order.

candy	_____	fifty	_____
apple	_____	ten	_____
salt	_____	thirty	_____
fruit	_____	five	_____
orange	_____	twenty	_____

over	_____	fudge	_____
beyond	_____	fig	_____
across	_____	feather	_____
above	_____	fuss	_____
toward	_____	fist	_____

balloon	_____	coat	_____
wagon	_____	hat	_____
puppet	_____	cap	_____
baby	_____	goat	_____
rabbit	_____	four	_____

pay	_____	Tim	_____
peach	_____	Jane	_____
pave	_____	Alice	_____
pencil	_____	Joe	_____
puddle	_____	Henry	_____

bed	_____
bead	_____
bear	_____
bet	_____
beef	_____

4

ABC ORDER

Arrange these words in alphabetical order to form complete sentences.

Punctuate each sentence correctly.

1. crashed the a tollgate car near

    _____

2. lime does pie Ethel like

    _____

3. play Beth can tennis Aunt

    _____

4. wheels the yesterday eight moved wagon men

    _____

5. eight arrives Alice o'clock always at

    _____

6. straight eating to I before ran town

    _____

7. house David find slippers can his

    _____

8. tomorrow may all soccer boys play

    _____

9. not Carl's contains marshmallows cereal strawberries

    _____

Make two scrambled sentences of your own. Ask a classmate to arrange them correctly.

5

ABC ORDER

Your job is to deliver supplies in a large office building. To make your job easier and complete your work faster, arrange the names in alphabetical order. Next arrange them in numerical order according to the floors on which they are located.

Robbie's Boutique Company	5
Land Real Estate Company	10
Harry Watson, M.D.	2
Janet Myers, M.D.	9
Savings and Loan Association	6
Tallent & Slack Employment Agency	1
Paulson's Publishing Company	8
Armstrong Computer Center	3
Duke Accounting Agency	7
See-Through Optical Service	4

Name	Floor	Floor	Name

Choose two offices that are in the building and design signs to put on both office doors.

Arrange this list of story titles as they would be found in a table of contents:

"Baseball Joey"   —   Shari Townsend
"Little Bear"   —   Henrietta Brown
"Kittens Next Door" —   Gary White
"Mice in Trouble"   —   Bruce Dunbar
"Purple Balloons"   —   Jim Edge
"Big Top"   —   Richard Dickinson
"Lost Toys"   —   Randy Hall
"Mystery House"   —   Hank Swords
"Mars Monster"   —   Mary Moore

_____

_____

_____

_____

_____

_____

_____

_____

Arrange the list of stories in alphabetical order according to the author's last name.

ABC ORDER

Preparation Directions:

Write each student's first and last name on a piece of tag-board 3" square. Put the names in a small box.

Player directions:

Using the timer you will find in the center, arrange your classmates' names in alphabetical order, last name first, before the end of three minutes.

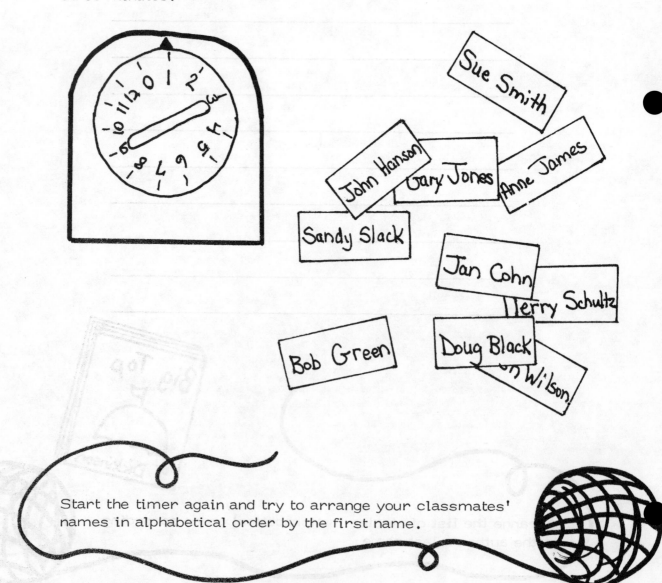

Start the timer again and try to arrange your classmates' names in alphabetical order by the first name.

A Big Cat (Alphabet Story)

Use your imagination to complete this alphabet story.
Start the first sentence with A, the next sentence with
B, and continue until you have written a sentence with
each letter of the alphabet.

_____

_____

_____

_____

_____

_____

_____

_____

_____

_____

_____

_____

_____

_____

_____

Make a picture of your Big Cat by tearing pieces of
construction paper and pasting them on drawing paper.

9

"Ah Dare You"

PURPOSE: | After completing this center, the student should be able to locate information in the encyclopedia.

MATERIALS: Illustration and title
             Encyclopedias
             Activity sheets
             Drawing paper

PROCEDURE: 1. Place all materials in center.

             2. Introduce the center to enable students to complete activities independently.

             3. Provide time for evaluation of each completed activity and record individual student progress.

             4. Make provision for filing or displaying completed activities.

CALLING
ALL
CATS

"AH DARE YOU"

Use the encyclopedia to locate information about
Abraham Lincoln.

1. What volume will you look in? _____

2. When was Abraham Lincoln born? _____

3. Where was he born? _____

4. What kind of family background did he have? _____

_____

_____

5. How was his education different from yours? _____

_____

_____

_____

6. Write a paragraph of at least seven sentences telling why
Abraham Lincoln was famous.

_____

_____

_____

_____

_____

_____

_____

7. What one thing do you remember best about him? _____

_____

_____

"AH DARE YOU"

Use the encyclopedia to locate this information.

1. Choose a person who is famous today. The person may be an inventor, president, athlete, author, musician, explorer or a scientist.
    Write the name of the person you have chosen here. _____

2. Write the letter of the volume you will use for information about this famous person. _____

3. When was this person born? _____

4. Where was he born? _____

5. Write a paragraph of at least five sentences that tell why this person is famous.

    _____

    _____

    _____

    _____

    _____

    _____

    _____

    _____

    _____

    _____

    _____

Pretend you are a famous person. Write a paragraph telling why you are famous.

"AH DARE YOU"

Use the encyclopedia to locate this information.

1. Choose a famous person who is no longer living to write about.   The famous person is

    _____

2. He (or she) is famous because _____

    _____

    _____

3. This person was born in _____ and died in _____ .

4. How many paragraphs did you find about this person? _____

5. Do you think the amount of information written about a person indicates how famous or important the person is? _____

6. Could this person be famous today? _____

7. Why? _____

    _____

    _____

Could I be famous in 1994?

Make a list of the questions you would ask this person if he were living today and you were a newspaper reporter interviewing him.

"AH DARE YOU"

Use the encyclopedia to locate this information.

1.   Select a famous person you want to find out more about. Write his name here.

   _____

2.   Write a report in your own words using the information from the encyclopedia. Be sure to include the most important facts about the person.

   _____

   _____

   _____

   _____

   _____

   _____

   _____

   _____

   _____

   _____

   _____

   _____

Using the large sheet of paper provided, lie down on it face up, and have a classmate outline around you. Draw your famous person in the outline.

? Compound Confusion ?

PURPOSE:
<blockquote>After completing this center, the student should be able to recognize and use compound words.</blockquote>

MATERIALS:
Illustration and title
Pencils and Crayons
Writing paper
Drawing paper
Books
5" x 8" sheet of tagboard

PROCEDURE:

1. Make game according to directions given in "Calling All Cats" activity.

2. Place all materials in the center.

3. Introduce the center to enable the student to complete activities independently.

4. Provide time for evaluation of each completed activity and record individual student progress.

5. Make provisions for filing or displaying completed activities.

COMPOUND CONFUSION

Game Activity

Materials:

1. Make a card from a piece of tagboard 5" x 8".
   Using two columns, print the first part of the
   compound word in the first column and the other
   half in the second column.

Directions:

1. Two players place this card between them.

2. The first player to write all the compound words wins.

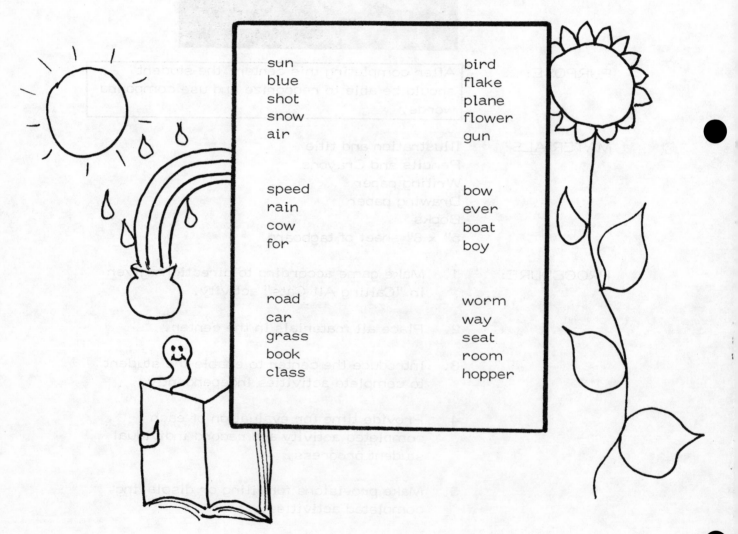

sun	bird
blue	flake
shot	plane
snow	flower
air	gun
speed	bow
rain	ever
cow	boat
for	boy
road	worm
car	way
grass	seat
book	room
class	hopper

COMPOUND CONFUSION

Match these words to make compound words.

pan	up
check	sauce
summer	cakes
flash	time
apple	light

ball	room
bed	field
where	day
birth	mate
play	ever

blue	bow	police	man
rain	knob	eye	bee
door	ball	snow	truck
snow	berries	fire	glasses
foot	man	bumble	shoes

suit	set	card	board
sea	book	class	board
up	house	every	butter
doll	shells	peanut	room
scrap	case	chalk	one

pan + cakes = pancakes

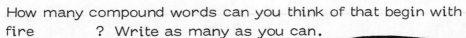

How many compound words can you think of that begin with fire_____? Write as many as you can.

17

COMPOUND CONFUSION

Here are some compound words, but they have lost their partners. Add the word needed to make them compound words again.

fire_____   _____bird

____plane   snow_____

sun_____   _____man

butter____   chalk____

____ever   him_____

____light   ____ache

ship_____   _____writer

_____boy   book_____

____melon   _____day

what____   back____

_____ware   fisher____

_____walk   rail_____

Select a book from the center and find ten compound words. List them here.

_____ _____ _____

_____ _____ _____

_____

COMPOUND CONFUSION

When two words are put together to form one word, it is called a compound word. Underline all the compound words in this story and then write the two words which make up each compound in the spaces below the story.

The Baseball Game

Yesterday afternoon my grandfather took us to the stadium for a baseball game. We were overjoyed when he called to invite us, but we worried when it started raining. The storm started to clear and as the sun came out, a rainbow was seen. Grandpa picked us up in a taxicab and we got to the game early. We had time to buy some popcorn and crackerjacks; then we found our seats. The baseball game was exciting and one ballplayer hit a home run. Our team won. On our way home we stopped for a milkshake. Boy, did we have fun!

1. _____   8. _____

2. _____   9. _____

3. _____   10. _____

4. _____   11. _____

5. _____   12. _____

6. _____   13. _____

7. _____   14. _____

15. _____

Write a paragraph telling about some place you'd like your grandfather to take you.

COMPOUND CONFUSION

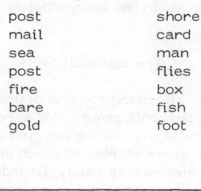

Match these words by drawing lines to make compound words. Then write a paragraph using all the compound words.

post	shore
mail	card
sea	man
post	flies
fire	box
bare	fish
gold	foot

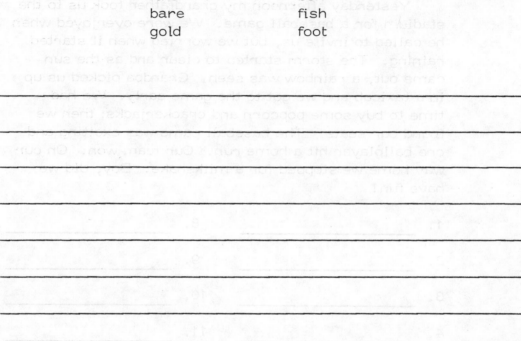

_____

_____

_____

_____

_____

_____

_____

_____

Draw a picture illustrating your paragraph. In your drawing include pictures of all the compound words at the top of your sheet.

Following the example given, put as many spokes as you can on each wheel.

somewhere   somewhat   somebody
        something   some   someone

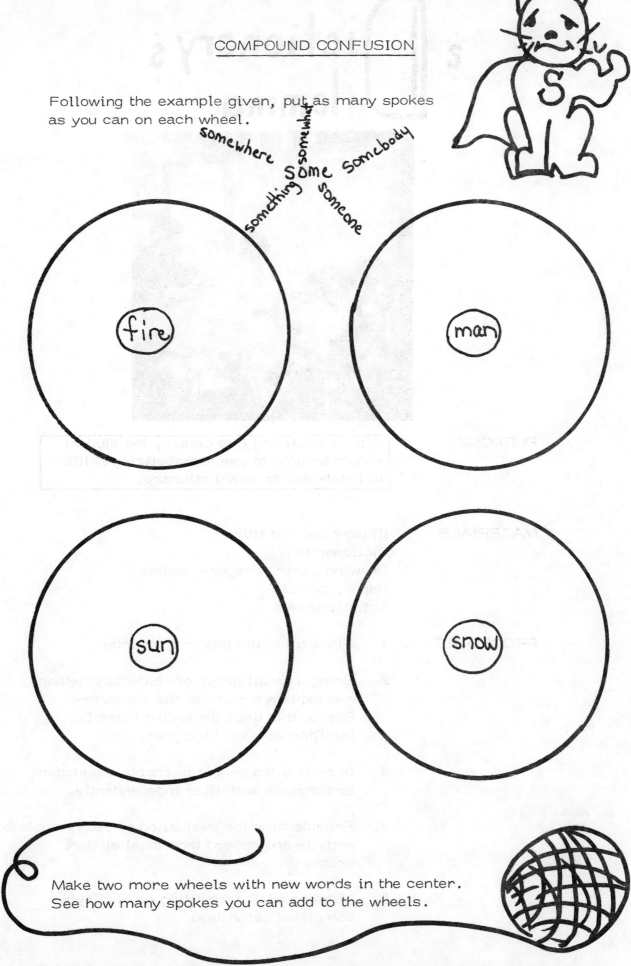

fire

man

sun

snow

Make two more wheels with new words in the center.
See how many spokes you can add to the wheels.

¿Dictionary¿ Dilemma

PURPOSE:
After completing this center, the student should be able to use alphabetizing skills to locate words in a dictionary.

MATERIALS:
Illustration and title
Dictionaries
Drawing paper, crayons, paints
Paper, pencils
Activity sheets

PROCEDURE:

1. Place all materials in the center.

2. Bring a small group of students together and explain the use of the dictionary. Repeat this until the entire class is familiar with the dictionary.

3. Introduce the center to enable the student to complete activities independently.

4. Provide time for evaluation of each completed activity and record individual student progress.

5. Make provision for filing or displaying completed activities.

DICTIONARY DILEMMA

The words in a dictionary are arranged in alphabetical order. Number the words in each list according to which comes first, second, and third in the dictionary.

___ oat   ___ easy

___ orange   ___ eager

___ ostrich ___ eat

___ kitten   ___ famous   ___ breakfast   ___ doll

___ puppy   ___ take   ___ bacon   ___ dance

___ mice   ___ cub   ___ beef   ___ dinner

___ sprite   ___ pair   ___ step   ___ though

___ swim   ___ plain   ___ street   ___ tough

___ stop   ___ prison   ___ stream   ___ thought

___ always   ___ zoo   ___ which   ___ crayon

___ air   ___ zebra   ___ whale   ___ candle

___ apple   ___ zero   ___ whole   ___ cook

___ bake   ___ walk   ___ church   ___ lime

___ bag   ___ wall   ___ chin   ___ limb

___ bark   ___ wait   ___ chug   ___ limit

DICTIONARY DILEMMA

Guide words are found at the top of every dictionary page and they are printed in darker type. The guide word on the left is the first word on the page, and the guide word on the right is the last word on the page.

Find these words in the dictionary and write the two guide words that are on that page.

Guide Words:

1. winter   _____   _____

2. jam   _____   _____

3. divide   _____   _____

4. peanut   _____   _____

5. reptile   _____   _____

6. giraffe   _____   _____

7. book   _____   _____

8. music   _____   _____

9. tornado   _____   _____

10. electric   _____   _____

Write your favorite food here. _____

Look up this word and write the two guide words on the page.

_____   _____

24

DICTIONARY DILEMMA

Cross out the word in each group that doesn't belong.
Put the other words in alphabetical order.

Vegetables		Animals	
beans	_____	squirrel	_____
squash	_____	leopard	_____
asparagus	_____	canary	_____
cantaloupe	_____	rhinoceros	_____
lettuce	_____	skunk	_____
carrots	_____	rabbit	_____

States		Communication	
Wyoming	_____	telephone	_____
Maine	_____	talk	_____
Italy	_____	telegram	_____
Florida	_____	radio	_____
Tennessee	_____	book	_____
Ohio	_____	riding	_____

Think of five words about transportation. Add one word
that is not related to transportation. Write the list and
ask someone in the center to find the word that doesn't
belong.

_____
_____
_____
_____
_____

DICTIONARY DILEMMA

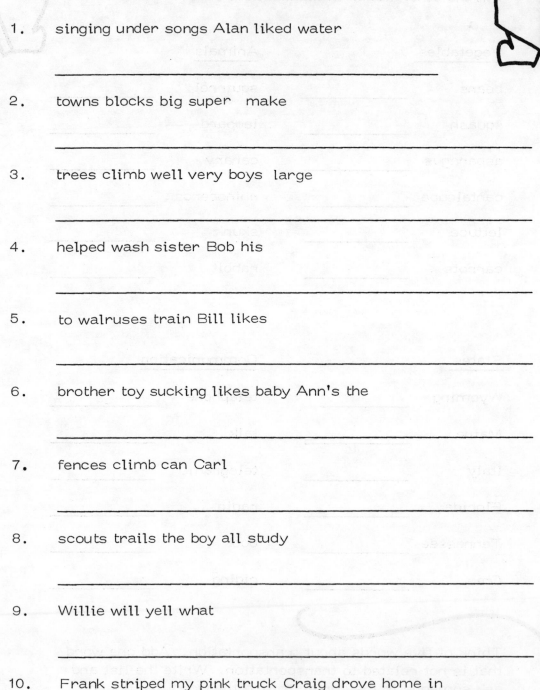

Write each list of words in alphabetical order. When the list is in the correct order, it will make a sentence.

1. singing under songs Alan liked water

    _____

2. towns blocks big super make

    _____

3. trees climb well very boys large

    _____

4. helped wash sister Bob his

    _____

5. to walruses train Bill likes

    _____

6. brother toy sucking likes baby Ann's the

    _____

7. fences climb can Carl

    _____

8. scouts trails the boy all study

    _____

9. Willie will yell what

    _____

10. Frank striped my pink truck Craig drove home in

    _____

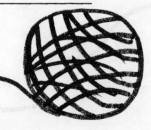

Write a sentence about cats that would be in alphabetical order like the ones above.

DICTIONARY DILEMMA

Look up each of these words in the dictionary and
write the two guide words that are on the same page.
Write the number of syllables in each guide word.

1. walrus   _____ ___ _____ ___

2. wallaby   _____ ___ _____ ___

3. strainer   _____ ___ _____ ___

4. preposition   _____ ___ _____ ___

5. pretzel   _____ ___ _____ ___

6. finch   _____ ___ _____ ___

7. croquet   _____ ___ _____ ___

8. aquaduct   _____ ___ _____ ___

9. larceny   _____ ___ _____ ___

10. frustrate   _____ ___ _____ ___

11. evacuate   _____ ___ _____ ___

12. demolish   _____ ___ _____ ___

Write the first names of all the students working with you
in this center. _____

_____

Now alphabetize their names and put the number of syllables
in each name. _____ ___, _____ ___,

_____ ___, _____ ___,

DICTIONARY DILEMMA

Look up each of these words in the dictionary and write the two guide words that are on the same page. Write a sentence using one of the guide words.

1. remember   _____   _____

_____

2. parasite   _____   _____

_____

3. illness   _____   _____

_____

4. dirigible   _____   _____

_____

5. catnip   _____   _____

_____

6. barnacle   _____   _____

_____

7. pressure   _____   _____

_____

Think of five words that begin with the letter M. Write them here. _____ _____ _____

_____ _____

Put these words in alphabetical order. _____

_____   _____   _____   _____

If these were the only words on a dictionary page, what would the two guide words be? _____   _____

DICTIONARY DILEMMA

Look up each underlined word in the dictionary.
Answer each question with a complete sentence.

1. What is a pomegranate? _____

   _____

2. Vanilla comes from what plant? _____

   _____

3. Where do peanuts grow? _____

   _____

4. What is a ferocious dog? _____

   _____

5. If you had a coat that was azure, what color would it be?

   _____

6. If you had a sabot, where would you wear it? _____

   _____

7. What could you do with currency? _____

   _____

8. If you ate lotus, how would you feel? _____

   _____

9. What would you use to play lacrosse? _____

   _____

10. A harpsichord is like what musical instrument? _____

Draw a person wearing a toga.

Extra! Extra! Read All About It!

PURPOSE: After completing this center, the student
            should be able to locate information in the
            encyclopedia.

MATERIALS: Illustration and title
            Encyclopedias
            Activity sheets
            Boxes, paints, drawing paper
            Construction paper, crayons

PROCEDURE: 1. Prepare corner for displaying city made
                from boxes as explained in option in "Cool
                Cat" activity. Place all materials in center.

            2. Introduce the center to enable the student
                to complete activities independently.

            3. Provide time for evaluation of each
                completed activity and record individual
                student progress.

            4. Make provision for filing or displaying
                completed activities.

EXTRA! EXTRA! READ ALL ABOUT IT!

Use the encyclopedia to find this information.

1. On what continent is the United States located?

    _____

2. Name the countries on this continent.

    _____   _____

    _____   _____

    _____   _____

3. Who discovered America? _____

4. When was America discovered? _____

5. What was the first state and last state to join the United States?

    _____   _____

6. Who was the first president of the United States? _____

7. Who is the president of the United States today? _____

8. What is the capital of the United States? _____

9. What types of climate are in the United States?

    _____   _____

    _____   _____

10. For what products is the United States well-known?

    _____   _____

    _____   _____

11. List some customs that are found only in the United States.

    _____

    _____

EXTRA! EXTRA! READ ALL ABOUT IT!

Use the encyclopedia to find this information.

1. If you could go to any large city in the United States, where would you go?

   _____

2. Use the encyclopedia to learn more about this city. What volume would you use?

   _____

3. List three interesting facts about this city.

   (1) _____

   _____

   (2) _____

   _____

   (3) _____

   _____

4. In what state is this city located? _____

5. Would you like to live in this city? _____

6. Why? _____

   _____

   _____

Using one of the boxes, build something that you would find in this city. Paint your model building and add it to the classroom city.

EXTRA! EXTRA! READ ALL ABOUT IT!

Use the encyclopedia to find this information.

1. If you could go to any state in the United States, where would you most like to go?

    _____

2. What volume of the encyclopedia would you use to find information about your state?

    _____

3. What is the state flower? _____

4. What is the state bird? _____

5. List three reasons why you would like to visit this state.

    (1) _____

    _____

    (2) _____

    _____

    (3) _____

    _____

6. Would you like to live in this state? _____

7. Why? _____

    _____

    _____

    _____

Make this state's flag. Use construction paper to make your flag. When you finish, display your flag on the bulletin board.

EXTRA! EXTRA! READ ALL ABOUT IT!

Use the encyclopedia to find this information.

1.   If you could go to any country in the world, where
      would you most like to go?

      _____

2.   What volume of the encyclopedia would you use
      to find information about this country?

      _____

3.   What is the capital of this country?

      _____

4.   What language do most of the people living in this country
      speak?

      _____

5.   List three ways this country is different from the United
      States.

      (1) _____

      _____

      (2) _____

      _____

      (3) _____

      _____

Look in the encyclopedia and find what type of clothing is
worn in this country. Hint: You may have to use a different
encyclopedia. Draw a picture of a person living in this
country showing the kind of clothes he might wear. Add
background scenery that you might expect to see in this
country.

34

Extraordinary

PURPOSE:

After completing this center, the student should be able to recognize and write personal and indefinite pronouns.

MATERIALS:
Illustration and title
Tagboard
Activity sheets
Game

PROCEDURE:

1. Make game cards and board according to "Super Cat" directions.

2. Place all materials in the center.

3. Introduce the center to enable the student to complete the activities independently.

4. Provide time for evaluation of each activity and record individual progress.

5. Make provision for filing or displaying completed activities.

EXTRAORDINARY ELF

Underline the subject in each sentence.
Write personal or indefinite pronoun to describe it.

1. We went to see the circus on my birthday. _____

2. Everybody was watching the football game. _____

3. No one in our room rides a bus to school. _____

4. It has a black and white spot on its head. _____

5. Somebody ran to tell us the good news. _____

6. They rode on the float in the parade. _____

7. He heard the animal cry for help. _____

8. Anyone may come to the party at school. _____

9. I am studying grammar in English. _____

10. Anybody could enjoy planting a garden. _____

11. They plan to visit the museum. _____

12. Something flew in the window and hit my desk. _____

13. Nothing was in the package that we found. _____

14. You are the first person to arrive at school. _____

15. Someone brought some pretty flowers. _____

Personal
Pronoun

or

Indefinite
Pronoun

EXTRAORDINARY ELF

Rewrite each sentence below. Use a personal pronoun to replace the subject in each sentence.

Example: The <u>robin</u> made a nest in the tree.
<u>It</u> made a nest in the tree.

1.   The man in the blue suit spoke to us.

_____

2.   His mother helped us bake a cake.

_____

3.   The children were playing football at school.

_____

4.   Roy was reading an interesting book about dinosaurs.

_____

5.   The rain helps flowers to grow.

_____

6.   Shepherds have to spend many hours hunting lambs.

_____

7.   The broken pencil was on the desk.

_____

8.   Sally answered the question correctly.

_____

9.   The mailman delivered the package on my birthday.

_____

Select a friend to help you think of five nouns. Take turns substituting a personal pronoun for each noun.

EXTRAORDINARY ELF

Steve		Joe		he		it
Mary	car	school		she	I	they
dog		cat		we		you

Look at the nouns and personal pronouns above.

Write a sentence with each noun. Under each sentence with a noun, write a sentence changing the noun to a personal pronoun.

Example: Words – (Steve – he)

1. Steve is my friend at school.
    _____

    He is my friend at school.
    _____

2. _____

    _____

3. _____

    _____

4. _____

    _____

5. _____

    _____

6. _____

    _____

7. _____

    _____

Using a noun in the subject, write five sentences about people or things in the room. Write the sentences again changing the noun to a personal pronoun.

EXTRAORDINARY ELF

Game Activity – Directions:

1. Two players are needed for this game.
2. Draw a card – if the question is answered correctly, move ahead one square.
3. If you land on a space with directions, be sure to follow them.
4. The first player to reach the "finish" wins!

EXTRAORDINARY ELF

Put these questions on small pieces of tagboard to
be used as the game cards.

Margaret broke her leg.
Change the subject to a personal pronoun.

She practiced her music.
What is the subject of this sentence?

Name one indefinite pronoun.

The ball hit me.
Change the subject to an indefinite pronoun.

Name two personal pronouns.

Everything got wet during the rain.
Change the subject to another indefinite pronoun.

They came in a box.
Change the subject to another personal pronoun.

Name three words that can be added to all indefinite pronouns.

Name the seven personal pronouns.

On the blank pieces of tagboard, make up two
questions to use with the game.

Fishing for Nouns

PURPOSE:

> After completing this center, the student should be able to recognize and use nouns in sentences.

MATERIALS:
Illustration and title
Activity sheets, writing paper
Wooden block for die
Tagboard
Box for puzzles

PROCEDURE:

1. Make fish bowl and fish according to directions given in "Cool Cat" activity. Make game as explained in "Super Cat" activity. Provide a box for puzzles to use with optional activity on "Smarty Cat" activity.

2. Place all materials in center.

3. Introduce the center to enable the student to complete activities independently.

4. Provide time for evaluation of each completed activity and record individual student progress.

5. Make provision for filing or displaying completed activities.

FISHING FOR NOUNS

Put the words from the list below in the right boxes.

Nouns	Not Nouns

necktie   hot
put   penny   examination
apples   quickly   silly
slept   postman

Draw a ring around the noun or nouns in each sentence.

1.   Her coat is pretty.

2.   My dog plays with me.

3.   His father is big.

4.   A watermelon has seeds.

5.   My mother made me a dress.

6.   Our house is near the river.

7.   The ship sailed into the harbor.

8.   Those boys ran fast.

Write a noun to complete each subject.

1.   The _____ ran down the road.

2.   His _____ fell off the bicycle.

3.   The _____ was juicy.

4.   My _____ is torn.

FISHING FOR NOUNS

Make a fishbowl out of tagboard. Cut out center and cover it with plastic wrap. Cut shapes of fish from tagboard, and on each fish write a common noun. Put fish in fishbowl and place on bulletin board or in center.

Directions:

Catch a fish and write a sentence using each noun as the subject or part of the subject.

Ideas to use on fish:

money

bus	weather
family	sapphire
story	camp
neighbor	house
eyes	inventor
reindeer	child
cloth	archaeologists
cake	adventure

toy

boy

shoe

Sombrero

Look around the classroom and list five common nouns. Make a sentence with each one.

FISHING FOR NOUNS

Nouns are names of persons, places, or things.
In this puzzle you must add and subtract letters to
make a list of nouns that live in the sea.

1.   woi – oi + hi – i + age – ge + l + ey – y

2.   stay – ay + i + ing – i + re – e + ays – s

3.   ijk – ik + def – df + ll + yes – es + fun – un + his – h + h

4.   act – at + out – ut + rat – at + a + let – et

5.   add – ad + nop – np + lip – i + hen – en + ing – g

6.   ask – ak + pqr – pr + you – yo + i + day – ay

7.   step – ep + at – t + are – ae + for – or + is + hat – at

1. _____

2. _____

3. _____

4. _____

5. _____

6. _____

7. _____

Make up a puzzle for something else you might find in
the sea. Put it in the puzzle box and let your classmates
try to guess what it is.

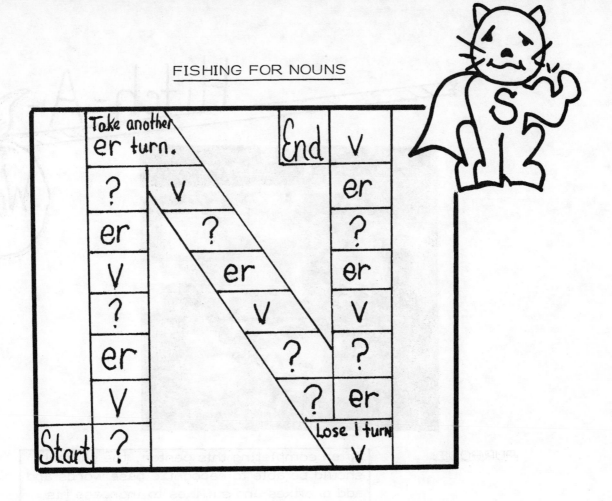

Use bottle caps for markers. Use one small square of wood as die. Put 1, 2, 3 and 4 dots on the four sides. Put words on 2" square pieces of tagboard.

This game is for two or three players.

The first player rolls the die and moves the number of spaces shown on the die. If the space is marked ? he must ask a question using the noun he draws as a subject. If the space is marked v he must change the noun to a verb. If the space is marked er he must use the noun in a sentence, but add er to the noun.

Example: talk _?_   Did you have a talk with her?
             dream _v_   I dream every night.
             hiker _er_ Jim is a good hiker.

Ideas to use on cards:

race	fight	sleep	run	park	walk	play
drive	step	help	slice	buy	move	camp
sing	paint	farm	build	mix		

Take the same noun cards and make another game.

45

Hitch-A-Word

PURPOSE: After completing this center, the student
             should be able to recognize base words and
             add prefixes and suffixes to increase his
             word usage.

MATERIALS: Illustration and title
             Writing paper, pencils
             Activity sheets

PROCEDURE: 1. Place all materials in the center.

             2. Introduce the center to enable the student
                 to complete activities independently.

             3. Provide time for evaluation of each
                 activity and record individual student
                 progress.

             4. Make provisions for filing or displaying
                 completed activities.

HITCH-A-WORD

A prefix is several letters added in front of a base word. Here are two: re and un. Un means not, and re means to do again.

Add the right prefix to each word to put in the sentences.

1.   Dad had to _____ the old lock. (place)

2.   This paper is messy; please _____ it. (copy)

3.   _____ your bike so you can ride it. (chain)

4.   If you want more milk, I will _____ it. (fill)

5.   We will _____ our room tomorrow. (paint)

6.   My mother likes to _____ paper. (use)

7.   Firecrackers can be _____. (safe)

8.   That story is so good I will _____ it. (tell)

9.   _____ the box so we can mail it. (seal)

10. _____ means to take the cover off. (cover)

11. I _____ my shoes before I take them off. (tie)

12. Mary helps Mother _____ the dishwasher each night. (load)

13. The story was so interesting that I _____ it. (read)

14. The policeman will _____ the traffic while the highway is being completed. (route)

15. The soup was not good, so I will _____ it. (cook)

47

HITCH-A-WORD

Suffixes are one or more letters added at the end of a base word. Here are two: <u>less</u> and <u>ful</u>.

Someone who is careless is without care.
Someone who is careful is full of care.

Answer these riddles by adding less or ful to the words.

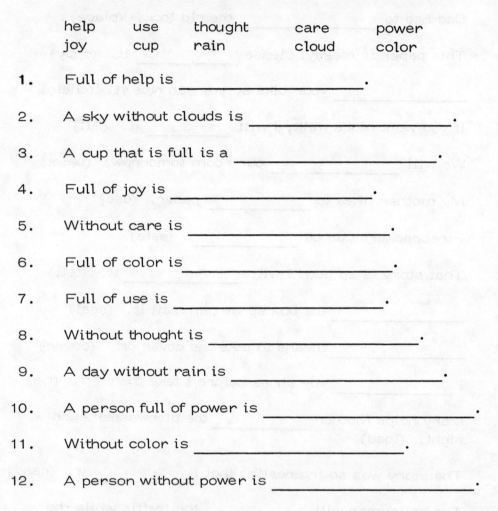

help	use	thought	care	power
joy	cup	rain	cloud	color

1. Full of help is _____.

2. A sky without clouds is _____.

3. A cup that is full is a _____.

4. Full of joy is _____.

5. Without care is _____.

6. Full of color is _____.

7. Full of use is _____.

8. Without thought is _____.

9. A day without rain is _____.

10. A person full of power is _____.

11. Without color is _____.

12. A person without power is _____.

Write the words that are the opposite of these:

joyful	colorful
helpless	watchful
careless	sleepful
thoughtful	useful
restful	hopeful
powerless	

HITCH-A-WORD

Match the same base words even though suffixes or prefixes have been added.

look	tries	weave	spied
slide	looking	sun	weaving
carry	tracing	spy	smiles
try	sliding	smile	tripping
trace	carries	trip	sunned

help	restless	safe	shorter
thought	useless	clean	unsafe
rest	thoughtful	able	newer
power	helpless	short	unable
use	powerful	new	cleanest

place	recopy	behave	amazement
chain	replace	amaze	misbehave
copy	unchain	part	department

Select four words with prefixes or suffixes added, and write four sentences using them. Illustrate the sentences.

HITCH-A-WORD

Write the base word on the line, using one letter for each dash. Every letter that has two dashes is part of a special code. See if you can figure it out!

1. helpful   — — = —

2. recount   — = — — —

3. smaller   — — — — =

4. fullest   — — = —

5. climbing   — — = — —

6. sleepless   — — — — =

7. opened   = — — —

8. copying   — — = —

9. suddenly   = — — — — —

10. darker   — = — —

11. warmest   — — = —

12. endless   = — —

13. graceful   = — — — —

14. longest   — = — —

15. coloring   — — — = —

16. handful   — — — =

Code:

= = = = = = = = = = = = = = = =
1 2 3 4 5 6 7 8 9 10 11 12 13 14 15 16

HITCH-A-WORD

Underline the base word in each word. Then use a
prefix or suffix to make a different word.

1. sunny	_____	15. planted	_____
2. nearest	_____	16. restless	_____
3. brighter	_____	17. cranky	_____
4. safely	_____	18. alarmed	_____
5. unhappy	_____	19. earliest	_____
6. locked	_____	20. shapeless	_____
7. sweetly	_____	21. fatten	_____
8. muddier	_____	22. greener	_____
9. dislike	_____	23. nibbling	_____
10. undecided	_____	24. raised	_____
11. dissatisfy	_____	25. careless	_____
12. patiently	_____	26. unsure	_____
13. bigger	_____	27. discontent	_____
14. sparkling	_____	28. rainy	_____

Have a contest with your friend using the words lock and
safe. See who can make the most words by adding prefixes
or suffixes.

Hooked on Sentences

PURPOSE: After completing this center, the student should be able to recognize and write complete sentences and use correct punctuation.

MATERIALS: Illustration and title
Poster board
Crayons
Activity sheets
Pencils
Sunday comics

PROCEDURE: 1.   Make Domino Game according to directions given in "Super Cat" activity.

2.   Place all materials in the center.

3.   Introduce the center to enable the student to complete activities independently.

4.   Provide time for evaluation of each completed activity and record individual student progress.

5.   Make provision for filing or displaying completed activities.

6.   Make a class booklet with the "Smarty Cat" comics.

HOOKED ON SENTENCES

Write each sentence again using capital letters, periods and question marks as needed.

1. hank is my best friend

    _____

2. we went to see Mary Poppins last night

    _____

3. where is your spelling book

    _____

4. the boys were flying kites in the empty field

    _____

5. i did my homework while watching television

    _____

6. have you ever eaten a mango

    _____

7. can you play the piano

    _____

8. my sister and i wash the dishes every night

    _____

9. when it snowed we made an igloo

    _____

10. may i have a piece of candy

    _____

HOOKED ON SENTENCES

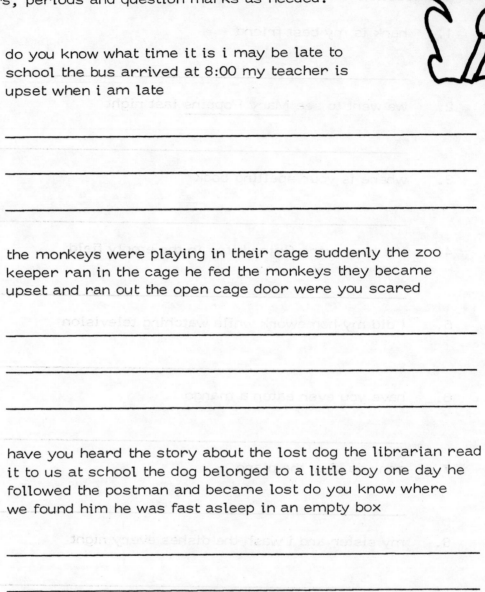

Correct each of the following paragraphs using capital letters, periods and question marks as needed.

do you know what time it is i may be late to
school the bus arrived at 8:00 my teacher is
upset when i am late

_____

_____

_____

the monkeys were playing in their cage suddenly the zoo
keeper ran in the cage he fed the monkeys they became
upset and ran out the open cage door were you scared

_____

_____

_____

have you heard the story about the lost dog the librarian read
it to us at school the dog belonged to a little boy one day he
followed the postman and became lost do you know where
we found him he was fast asleep in an empty box

_____

_____

_____

_____

Write a paragraph using these words. Use capital letters,
periods and question marks as needed.

lion   queen   truck   rule   clock

54

HOOKED ON SENTENCES

Read the Sunday comics in the center. Now write your own comics using your own name and characters. Be sure to write what the characters are saying in complete sentences and to use the correct punctuation.

Color your comics.

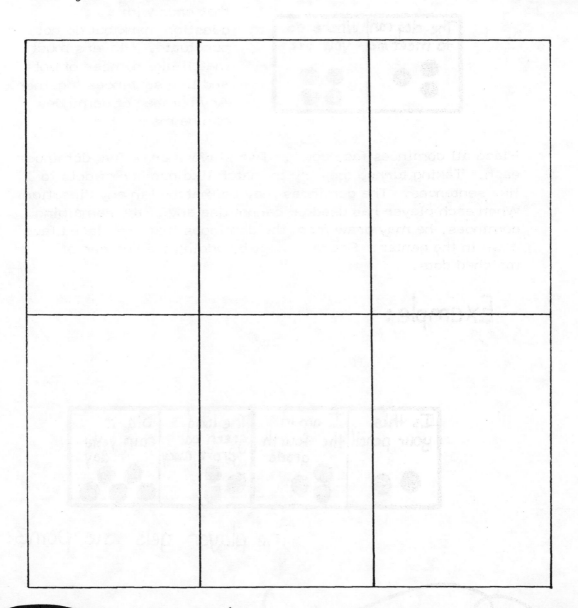

Add your comics to the class booklet and enjoy reading the ones your friends have completed.

Domino Sentences:

Cut pieces of poster board 4" x 2". Make a domino game by making dots on each piece of poster board. On each side of the domino write either a sentence that ends with

a period or a sentence that ends with a question mark but do not punctuate. Players must match like number of dots and like sentences together. Any number of dominoes can be made.

Place all dominoes face down. Two players draw five dominoes each. Taking turns, they try to match like number of dots to like sentences. The dominoes may be matched in any direction. When each player has used or cannot use any of the remaining dominoes, he may draw from the dominoes that are placed face down in the center. Score is kept by adding the number of matched dots.

Example:

The player gets six points.

Make up a game of your own using complete sentences. Challenge a friend to see if the game works!

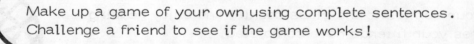

Sentence ideas to put on Dominoes
(Others may be added.)

We cooked hamburgers on the picnic.
Mother made my dress for the party.
The strong man can hold much more.
My friend plays baseball.
I ate a peanut butter sandwich.
The horse jumped over the fence.

The dog grabbed the bone.
Indians of different tribes had different customs.
My brother knew that author, too.
His adventures took him around the world.
The librarian helped me find a good book.
The snake makes a hissing sound.

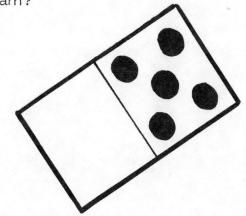

Can you repair my bicycle?
What language is spoken in Brazil?
Have you eaten dinner?
Where is the resource room?
Has Mary written a poem recently?
Is this your raincoat?

Did the cat catch the mouse?
Where did you buy your green airplane model?
What is your state bird?
Will you let me ride your motorbike?
What is your favorite kind of ice cream?
Are you going to the birthday party?

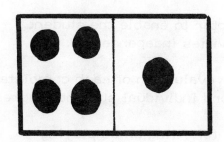

In Other Words

PURPOSE: After completing this center, the student should be able to identify synonyms and antonyms.

MATERIALS:
Illustration and title
Writing paper, pencil
Tagboard cards, crayons
Sheet of heavy plastic
Magic markers
Two bean bags

PROCEDURE:

1. Cut card-sized strips of tagboard or use index cards to print words for game, following directions given in "Calling All Cats" activity. Make game according to directions in optional activity.

2. Place all materials in center.

3. Introduce the center to enable the student to complete activities independently.

4. Provide time for evaluation of each completed activity and record individual student progress.

5. Make provisions for filing or displaying completed activities.

IN OTHER WORDS

1. Cut card-sized strips of tagboard or use index cards.

2. List one word below on each card.

weighty	healthy	frightened	heavy	
well	scared	okay	sea	
end	yes	ocean	finish	
crazy	store	stay	mad	shop
remain	father	uneven	evil	dad
odd	bad	movies	pair	forest
film	twin	woods	jump	permit
land	leap	let	ground	prepared
pull	total	fixed	tug	sum

Directions:

1. Choose two or three players for this game.

2. Shuffle the cards and deal seven cards to each player; spread the remaining cards face down.

3. One player begins by asking the player on his left for a synonym for one of his cards. If the player has it, he must give it to his opponent.

4. Every time a match is made, the player lays his match down in front of him.

5. If a player asks for a card and his opponent doesn't have it, he draws a card from the stack, and his opponent gets a turn.

6. After every card has been matched, the player with the most matches wins.

(This game is played much like the game Fish.)

This game could also be played with antonyms by changing half the cards.

IN OTHER WORDS

Mark these pairs of words with an "S" if they are synonyms; with an "A" if they are antonyms.

_____	quiet – still	_____ happy – sad
_____	pairs – twins	_____ open – closed
_____	forest – woods	_____ animal – fish
_____	wild – tame	_____ home – house
_____	scary – frightening	_____ empty – deserted
_____	below – under	_____ narrow – wide
_____	large – small	_____ well – sickly
_____	funny – silly	_____ huge – enormous
_____	tote – carry	_____ rainy – sunny
_____	tiny – wee	_____ pal – buddy
_____	sour – sweet	_____ sweets – candy
_____	appear – gone	_____ man – woman

Choose a pair of words above that are opposites. Draw a picture showing why they are opposite.

IN OTHER WORDS

Synonyms are two words that mean the same thing. Circle
the words in each row that mean the same thing as the first
word in the row.

1.	job	lazy	chore	task	play
2.	wild	tame	fierce	easy	lion
3.	wet	rainy	hot	cold	damp
4.	appear	under	show	hide	disappear
5.	hind	front	back	above	below
6.	narrow	open	wide	fat	limited
7.	glad	happy	sad	surprised	disappointed
8.	always	sometimes	never	ever	once-in-awhile
9.	quickly	slowly	rapidly	fast	lazy
10.	unable	won't	can't	able	skilled
11.	loosen	untie	tighten	close	freed
12.	many	several	one	none	all
13.	new	recent	old	fresh	aged
14.	scrub	filthy	clean	dirty	scour
15.	hungry	sick	thirsty	starved	full

Substitute a different word for <u>pretty</u> every time it appears
in this sentence to make the sentence more interesting.

My <u>pretty</u> sister gave me a <u>pretty</u> sweater wrapped
in a <u>pretty</u> package with a <u>pretty</u> bow.

IN OTHER WORDS

Substitute synonyms for as many words as you can in these sentences. Rewrite your new sentence underneath the old one.

1. Walking across the ground, I saw a few flowers.

    _____

    _____

2. The bee was looking for honey.

    _____

    _____

3. The boy swam slowly across the calm pool.

    _____

    _____

4. I bought a pretty shirt at the store.

    _____

    _____

5. All the boys ran across the grass to see the big elephant.

    _____

    _____

6. The baby was little and sad.

    _____

    _____

The words nice and happy are used so often that they are worn out. How many synonyms can you think of for nice?

_____

How about synonyms for happy? _____

62

IN OTHER WORDS

1. Section off into squares a 4' x 6' sheet of heavy plastic. Write one word per square using a magic marker.

Directions:

1. This game is to be played with two students or two teams.

2. The players may decide to play with synonyms or antonyms.

3. One at a time, the player throws the bean bag on a word. He is to supply a synonym (antonym) for the word the bag lands on.

4. One point is scored for each correct answer.

5. At the end of a specified time, the team with the most points wins.

immediately	sharp	crowd	halt	know	pure	scrap	under
generous	approve	rough	grasp	run	asleep	fancy	tight
aid	good	cheap	ignore	grow	friend	quiet	important
clear	now	restore	argue	pull	depart	strange	scurry

Leap Frog

PURPOSE:
> After completing this center, the student should be able to identify consonant blends.

MATERIALS:
Illustration and title
Pencils
Writing paper
Activity sheets

PROCEDURE:
1. Place all materials in the center.

2. Introduce the center to enable the student to complete activities independently.

3. Provide time for evaluation of each completed activity and record individual student progress.

4. Make provision for filing or displaying completed activities.

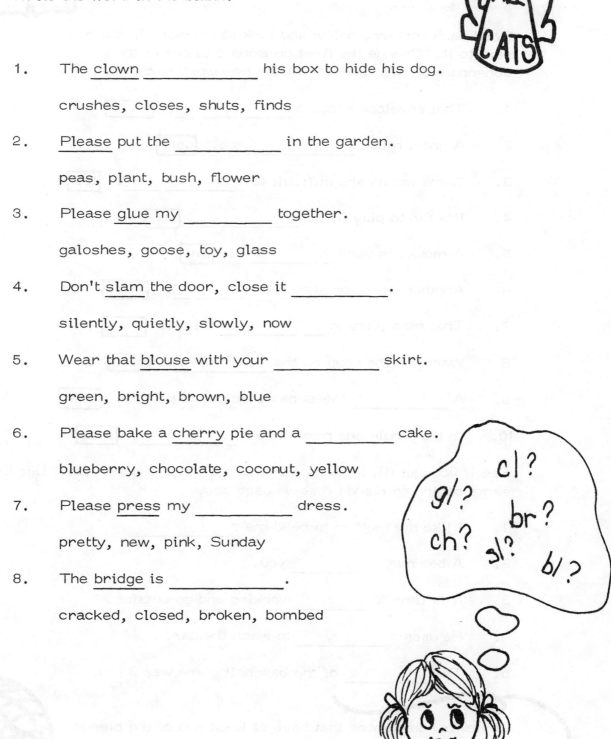

LEAP FROG

Pick out the one word under each sentence that has the same blend as the underlined word.

Write the word in the blank.

1.   The clown _____ his box to hide his dog.

      crushes, closes, shuts, finds

2.   Please put the _____ in the garden.

      peas, plant, bush, flower

3.   Please glue my _____ together.

      galoshes, goose, toy, glass

4.   Don't slam the door, close it _____.

      silently, quietly, slowly, now

5.   Wear that blouse with your _____ skirt.

      green, bright, brown, blue

6.   Please bake a cherry pie and a _____ cake.

      blueberry, chocolate, coconut, yellow

7.   Please press my _____ dress.

      pretty, new, pink, Sunday

8.   The bridge is _____.

      cracked, closed, broken, bombed

65

LEAP FROG

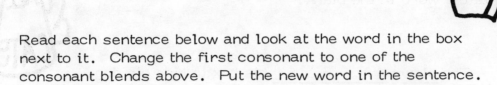

Underline the consonant blend in each word.

star   snake   spoon   smoke   scale

Read each sentence below and look at the word in the box next to it. Change the first consonant to one of the consonant blends above. Put the new word in the sentence.

1.   That envelope needs a _____.   camp

2.   A ghost might _____ me.   dare

3.   Some words are difficult to _____.   tell

4.   It's fun to play in the _____.   tow

5.   A mouse is very _____.   tall

6.   Another word for shovel is _____.   made

7.   That man likes to _____ a pipe.   poke

8.   Warm up the soup on the _____.   cove

9.   A _____ measures ounces and pounds.   pale

10.   In the jungle one might see a _____.   cake

See if you can fill in these sentences without a word clue. Use the same beginning blends that we used above.

1.   I like my mother to read me a _____.

2.   A bee may _____ you.

3.   It is time to _____ working and go outside.

4.   He uses a _____ to wash the car.

5.   The _____ of the baseball game was 3 – 0.

Write four sentences that have at least two of the blends in each sentence.

66

LEAP FROG

Read each sentence below and fill in the missing blend to make each word complete.

1.   On Halloween, he usually wears a ma_____.

2.   The king's son is a _____ince.

3.   Billy likes to _____imb trees.

4.   That _____uck was hauling dirt.

5.   If you can't find your way, you are lo_____.

6.   During school I often work at my de_____.

7.   The caboose is the last car on the _____ain.

8.   She has one sister and one _____other.

9.   When it is hot, it is fun to _____im.

10. If you have a question, please a_____.

11. It is polite to say _____ease.

12. A haunted house may have a gho_____.

13. This is the fir_____ cake I have ever baked.

14. _____ue is my favorite color.

15. I have a pair of ice _____ates.

16. She has a large green _____ant in her room.

With a friend choose one of the blends above and list as many words as possible which include that blend.

LEAP FROG

spr _ _ _

thr _ _ _

str _ _ _

scr _ _ _

Every word to the puzzle begins with a three-letter blend.

Across 1. We use it to swallow and talk.
        3. It helps wrap a package.
        5. A flavor of ice cream
        7. Another word for evergreen tree.
        9. A synonym for yell.
        11. It's used to keep flies out.
        13. A small cut.

Down   2. It is used for sewing.
        4. It's fun to run through during the summer.
        6. A number.
        8. Rows of colors are _____.
        10. A season of the year.
        12. A baseball term: 3 ____ make an out.

Make up your own crossword puzzle using blends.

Leo Lion

PURPOSE: | After completing this center, the student should be able to organize sentences to form a logical paragraph.

MATERIALS:
Illustration and title
Activity sheets
Sentence strips
Writing paper
Crayons
Drawing paper
Box

PURPOSE:

1. Place all materials in center. Write the six sentences in the "Calling All Cats" activity on strips of tagboard. Cut the sentences in three parts. Put the sentence strips in a box. (The student must put the parts of the sentences together to make a complete thought. The sentences will form a paragraph.) Make answer cards to enable the student to check his own sentences. The sentences can be color coded to make matching easier.

2. Introduce the center to enable the student to complete activities independently.

3. Provide time for evaluation of each completed activity and record individual student progress.

4. Make provision for filing or displaying completed activities.

LEO LION

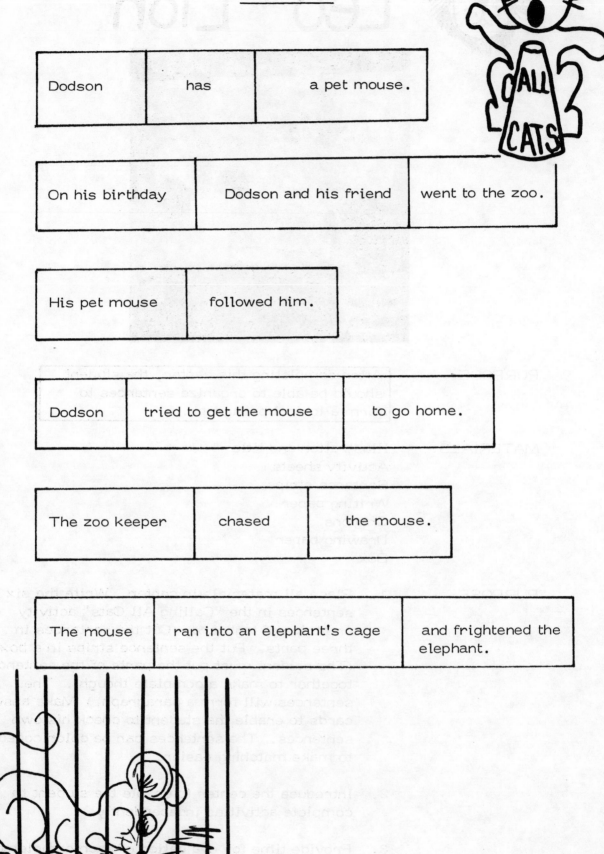

| Dodson | has | a pet mouse. |

| On his birthday | Dodson and his friend | went to the zoo. |

| His pet mouse | followed him. |

| Dodson | tried to get the mouse | to go home. |

| The zoo keeper | chased | the mouse. |

| The mouse | ran into an elephant's cage | and frightened the elephant. |

LEO LION

The groups of words below were once six sensible sentences. They have been mixed up so they no longer make sense. Put them back together so they form six sentences. Put together one group from each column. Write the sentences in paragraph form.

Group I	Group II	Group III
It was	the neon signs	it was Halloween
We watched	a cold night	all sorts of things
All around us	remembered	running down the street
Suddenly one of the boys	frightened and imagined	in a strange city
We became	saw a ghost	along the streets
Then we	the people were strolling	blink off and on

_____

_____

_____

_____

_____

_____

_____

_____

_____

Make a crayon resist illustrating the paragraph you have just written.

LEO LION

Mary wrote this story. Did she tell everything in the order that it happened? Think what happened first, and what happened following that. Write the paragraph in correct order.

After reading the directions, she emptied the cake mix into a bowl. Was Mother ever surprised! The recipe said to beat the batter for two minutes. Today was Mother's birthday. The cake looked gooey as she poured it in the pan. Mary wanted to surprise her Mother by baking a cake. Mary put all the ingredients together. After thirty minutes the cake was done and ready to eat.

_____

_____

_____

_____

_____

_____

_____

_____

Draw Mother's birthday cake.

LEO LION

Write a paragraph about a trip to the zoo.

_____

_____

_____

_____

_____

_____

_____

_____

Write a paragraph about an animal you saw in the zoo.

_____

_____

_____

_____

_____

_____

Write a paragraph about an imaginary animal you would
like to find in a zoo.

Look in the Book

PURPOSE: | After completing this center, the student should be able to use alphabetizing skills to locate information in the encyclopedia.

MATERIALS:
Illustration and title
Encyclopedias
Activity sheets
Pencils – Writing paper – Crayons – Paste
Drawing paper – Construction paper – Paints
Boxes

PROCEDURE:

1. Place all materials in the center.

2. Introduce the center to enable students to complete the activities independently.

3. Provide time for evaluation of each completed activity and record individual student progress.

4. Make provision for filing or displaying completed activities.

LOOK IN THE BOOK

Encyclopedias are in alphabetical order. What letter
is on the volume in which you must find this information?

1. Dinosaurs _____   4. Ontario _____
2. Benjamin Franklin _____   5. Space Travel _____
3. Indiana _____   6. Wheels _____

Find the answers by looking up the subjects in the encyclopedia.
Look for the word in CAPITAL LETTERS.

1. What is the capital of IDAHO? _____

2. The birth date of ELIZABETH II is _____ .

3. From what country did COLUMBUS sail? _____

4. What year did GEORGE WASHINGTON die? _____

Long articles are divided into sections called <u>Subsections</u>, or
<u>Subheads</u>. It is written in darker letters. Look in the encyclopedia
and find the first subhead after each main title. Write it beside the
title.

1. Moon _____

2. Insects _____

3. Tiger _____

4. Switzerland _____

5. Milk _____

6. Transportation _____

LOOK IN THE BOOK

1. What is your favorite wild animal?

   _____

2. Use the encyclopedia to locate information about this animal. What letter was on the volume in which you found this information?_____.

3. List three interesting facts about this animal.

   (1) _____

   _____

   (2) _____

   _____

   (3) _____

   _____

4. Where does this animal live? _____

   _____

   _____

5. What does this animal like to eat? _____

   _____

   _____

Draw a picture of your favorite wild animal.

LOOK IN THE BOOK

1. In the encyclopedia locate information about a second wild animal. The animal is _____.

2. What letter was on the volume in which you found this information? _____

3. List three ways that this animal is different from the first wild animal you learned about.

(1) _____

_____

_____

(2) _____

_____

_____

(3) _____

_____

Write an imaginary story about meeting this wild animal.

LOOK IN THE BOOK

1. In the encyclopedia locate information about a third wild animal you are interested in, and write its name here. _____

2. Describe its color. _____

    _____

    _____

3. Compare the size of this animal to an object you would find in your classroom.

    _____

    _____

4. Tell about your animal's environment. _____

    _____

    _____

5. Is your animal dangerous? _____
    What should fear your animal?

    _____

    _____

6. What is your animal's diet? _____

    _____

    _____

    _____

Draw or paint this animal in its natural environment.

Make - A - Thing

PURPOSE:
> After completing this center, the student should be able to develop picture images from the words he is using.

MATERIALS: Illustration and title

Tagboard cards   Crayons
Drawing paper   Pencils
Writing paper

PROCEDURE:
1. Print the nouns found on the following page on 1" x 2" pieces of tagboard. (Use both sides of the tagboard.)

2. Place illustration and title, drawing paper, tagboard cards and directions in the center.

3. Make time and space provisions for students who wish to share their work.

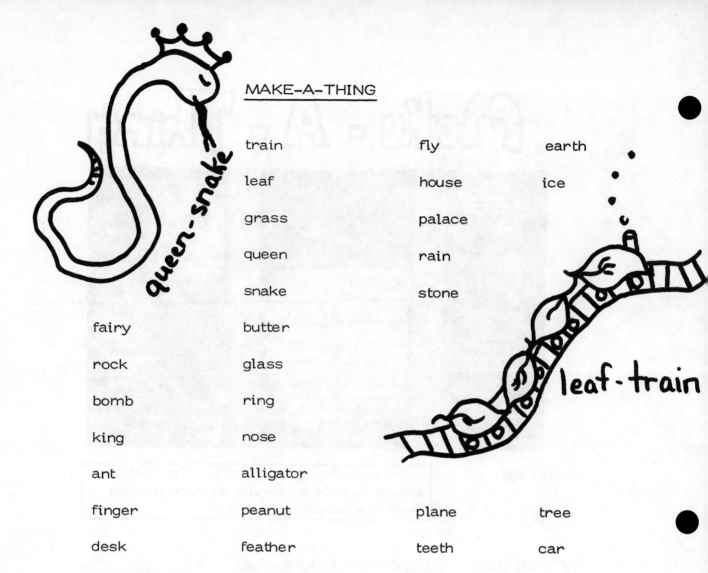

MAKE-A-THING

train	fly	earth
leaf	house	ice
grass	palace	
queen	rain	
snake	stone	

queen-snake

leaf-train

fairy	butter		
rock	glass		
bomb	ring		
king	nose		
ant	alligator		
finger	peanut	plane	tree
desk	feather	teeth	car

Add some of your own!

Directions:

1. Read all the words and then choose two words to put together. It may be a make-believe "thing".

2. On a sheet of drawing paper write the two words that you have matched. With crayons, draw a picture of your "thing".

3. Write a short story about your "thing".

Do another!

PURPOSE:

> After completing this center, the student
> should be able to follow written directions
> and to work independently.

MATERIALS: Illustration and title
Activity sheets
Crayons
Pencils

PROCEDURE:

1. Place all materials in center.

2. Verbally introduce the center to enable
   the student to complete activities independently.

3. Provide time for evaluation of each completed
   activity and record individual student progress.

4. Make provisions for filing or displaying
   completed activities.

81

MOUSETRAP

Can you follow directions? You will need your crayons to follow these directions:

1. Put a green star before anything that is <u>round</u>.
2. Put a red square before anything that is <u>heavy</u>.
3. Put a black triangle before anything that is <u>light</u>.
4. Put a blue circle before anything that is <u>tall</u>.

_____ rain drop	_____ hamburger
_____ metal pipe	_____ box of books
_____ potato chip	_____ cotton candy
_____ redwood tree	_____ Rocky Mountains
_____ radio tower	_____ steam shovel
_____ ring	_____ jaw breaker
_____ flag pole	_____ straight pin
_____ bicycle tire	_____ pencil
_____ tissue paper	_____ shark
_____ soccer ball	_____ dinosaur
_____ Empire State Building	_____ hippopotamus
_____ lollipop	_____ bottle cap

Look around the classroom and find one object that is <u>round</u>, one object that is <u>heavy</u>, one object that is <u>light</u>, and one object that is <u>tall</u>.

_____ round   _____ heavy

_____ light   _____ tall

MOUSETRAP

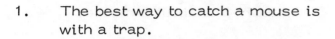

By following all directions carefully, you will find out if you are a good mouse catcher.

Circle the letter in the <u>yes</u> or <u>no</u> answer box you choose.

1.   The best way to catch a mouse is with a trap.

2.   Mice hate cheese.

3.   Mice are larger than cats.

4.   Mice are often gray.

5.   Mice always live in barns.

6.   Mice are rodents.

7.   Most mothers like mice.

	Yes	No
1.	T	E
2.	S	R
3.	C	A
4.	P	A
5.	R	P
6.	E	T
7.	L	D

What happened to the mouse?

What did you spell? _ _ _ _ _ _ _ _

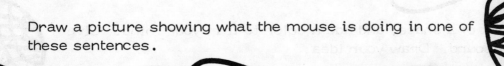

Draw a picture showing what the mouse is doing in one of these sentences.

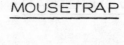

MOUSETRAP

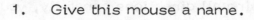

1. Give this mouse a name.

_____

Use your pencil to color his
ears gray. Add whiskers to
his face. Write two lines
that rhyme about a mouse.

_____

_____

2. This lollipop does not have a flavor.
What flavor would you make it?

_____

Color it the flavor you have chosen.
Draw a rectangle around the lollipop.

3. These plants are missing their flowers.
Draw the missing flowers. Circle the
flower on the right. Draw two insects
below that you might find near the flowers.

4. List three months that you think are
winter months.

_____   _____   _____

Draw three snowmen and label each one
a different winter month.

Think of a shape, and add a color to it in your mind. Give
it a sound. Draw your idea.

MOUSETRAP

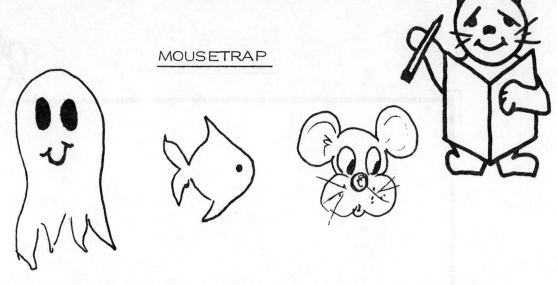

1. If a mouse likes a cat, put a X under the picture of the ghost.

2. If a ghost sometimes frightens people, draw a circle around the picture of the mouse.

3. If a mouse is usually gray and has long ears, underline the third word in this sentence.

4. If a mouse has short ears, put a piece of cheese by the mouse.

5. If a fish lives in water, underline this sentence.

6. If a ghost is real, draw a line from the ghost to the mouse.

7. If you can eat fish, make a smiling face after this sentence.

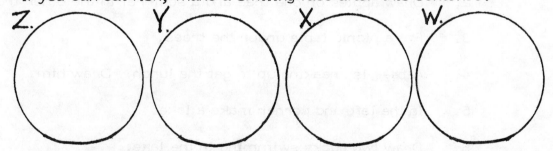

8. In the middle of Circle Z make a red circle.

9. Divide Circle Y in half, and write the first letter of your name on the line.

10. In Circle W, draw a silly face.

11. In Circle X, color one-fourth of the circle orange.

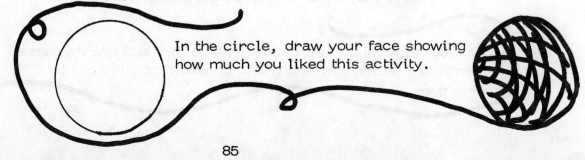

In the circle, draw your face showing how much you liked this activity.

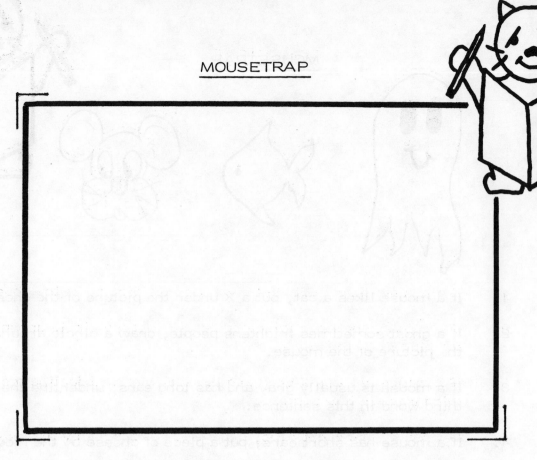

Create a picture by following these directions. Remember to color your picture.

1.   Make two trees in the middle of the picture frame.

2.   Draw apples on one tree and a squirrel in the other tree.

3.   Put a picnic table under the trees.

4.   A bear is sneaking up to get the lunch. Draw him.

5.   In the lefthand corner make a lake.

6.   Draw two ducks swimming in the lake.

7.   In the righthand corner, make a swimming pool.

8.   Draw a diving board at each end of the pool.

9.   Draw yourself in the picture.

10.   Finish your picture by drawing grass and the sky.

Do you think this would be a fun place to visit? Write three sentences telling why you would or would not like to visit this park.

MOUSETRAP

Help Ann follow this list of clues to find her birthday present. The first clue is under her bed. Draw a green path from Ann's bed to her dresser.

Go down the hall to the plant. Another clue says to look in the bathroom sink. Now go downstairs and look on top of the T.V.

Ann must still keep looking. Draw a line from the T.V. to the picture on the wall. Go on to the bookshelf and look in the red book. The next clue tells you to go to the kitchen and look in the oven.

Look under your kitchen chair, then in your cereal bowl. This clue tells Ann to go back to bed. There on Ann's bed is her gift. You have drawn it. What is it?

A. Ann's bed
B. Red book
C. Ann's dresser
D. The plant

E. Book shelf
F. Cereal bowl
G. Kitchen chair
H. Top of T.V.
I. Bathroom sink

J. Picture on the wall
K. The hall
L. Kitchen
M. Oven

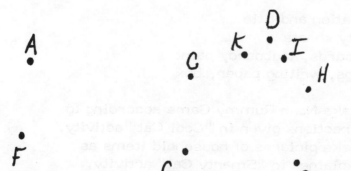

Color Ann's birthday present.

zzie Owl

PURPOSE: After completing this center, the student
            should be able to recognize and use proper
            nouns.

MATERIALS: Illustration and title
            Activity sheets
            Index cards, tagboard, paint
            Crayons, writing paper, box

PROCEDURE: 1. Make Noun Rummy Game according to
                directions given in "Cool Cat" activity.
                Make pictures of household items as
                explained in "Smarty Cat" activity.

            2. Place all materials in the center.

            3. Introduce the center to enable the student
                to complete activities independently.

            4. Provide time for evaluation of each
                completed activity and record individual
                student progress.

            5. Make provision for filing or displaying
                completed activities.

OZZIE OWL

Underline the proper nouns in the list below and write each correctly.

picnic	miss martin	johnny
sally	january	king
vegetable	elm street	charlotte's web
monday	leaves	mary
mr. jones	farmer	halloween

_____   _____   _____

_____   _____   _____

_____   _____   _____

Rewrite each sentence and capitalize the proper nouns.

1. A holiday in july is the fourth of july.

_____

_____

2. Last night dan and joe slept outdoors.

_____

_____

3. My favorite book is treasure island.

_____

_____

4. There goes mr. jones with his dog snoopy.

_____

_____

5. Every saturday I watch cartoons on television.

_____

_____

OZZIE OWL

Game: Noun Rummy
(for two players)

Write common nouns on index cards. From the stack
of cards placed face down, one player draws a card.
He must say a proper noun for the common noun that is
on the card. He continues to get additional turns until
he fails to give a proper noun for a common noun. When
all the cards have been drawn, the player with the most cards wins.

Common nouns for cards:

car	teacher	valley	song
boy	school	mountain	author
girl	mother	river	ocean
bird	city	movie	ship
tree	state	friend	astronaut
book	country	church	scientist
street	cat	pirate	airplane
explorer	bridge	newspaper	butterfly

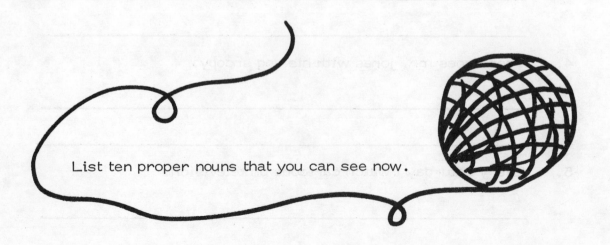

List ten proper nouns that you can see now.

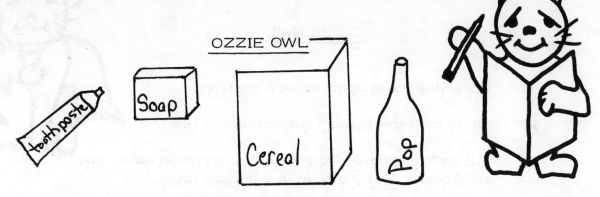

OZZIE OWL

Each needs a proper noun.

Pictures of all kinds of household items can be made out of tagboard and put on bulletin board in the center or put in a box. Label each picture with a common noun. The student must write a proper noun for each picture.

Ideas to put on pictures:

deodorant	lipstick
cereal	toothpaste
candy bar	mouthwash
cookies	perfume
gum	dishwashing liquid
soap	bubble bath

pop

Think of one more household item. Draw it, color it, and cut it out. Write the common noun on the picture and add it to the other pictures.

OZZIE OWL

1. Underline the subject in each sentence.

2. Write the noun in each subject on the line.

3. Put an X beside C if the noun is a common noun, and an X beside P if the noun is a proper noun.

1. The villagers listened quietly to the mayor.

   _____ C ____ P ____

2. Horses like to be ridden by children.

   _____ C ____ P ____

3. Robbie sang at church yesterday.

   _____ C ____ P ____

4. His father is a teacher in our school.

   _____ C ____ P ____

5. Mr. Johnson built an apartment building.

   _____ C ____ P ____

6. A fable is a story that has a moral.

   _____ C ____ P ____

7. Thanksgiving is always in November.

   _____ C ____ P ____

8. The boys and girls had a softball game.

   _____ C ____ P ____

Rewrite the sentences above. If the subject has a common noun, change it to a proper noun. If the subject has a proper noun, change it to a common noun.

OZZIE OWL

Write a story using one of the following ideas:

1.   The dream I had one night

2.   My trip to the zoo

3.   A visit to Grandmother's house

Try to include at least ten proper nouns in your story and underline each one.

_____

_____

_____

_____

_____

_____

_____

_____

_____

_____

_____

_____

With a friend, think of a common noun, give two clues, and see if he can give a proper noun for the word. Take turns playing this game until each person has had five turns.

Phonics Playground

PURPOSE: | After completing this center, the student should be able to differentiate between long and short vowel sounds.

MATERIALS: Illustration and title
             Activity sheets
             Tagboard
             Box for word cards

PROCEDURE: 1. Print the words listed in "Cool Cat" game
                 activity on 1" x 2" tagboard cards. Place
                 all materials in the center.

             2. Introduce the center to enable the student
                 to complete activities independently.

             3. Provide time for evaluation of each completed
                 activity and record individual student progress.

             4. Make provision for filing or displaying
                 completed activities.

PHONICS PLAYGROUND

Mark each vowel to show its long or short sound.

cage	a	lake	a	lake	a
pail	a	nail	a	rain	a
car	a	ball	a	bat	a
day	a	bay	a	way	a

mess	e	hem	e	pet	e
meat	e	heat	e	peach	e
men	e	these	e	pen	e
meet	e	beet	e	peel	e

Tim	i	fish	i	fire	i
tin	i	fine	i	fix	i
tie	i	fin	i	fir	i
tip	i	find	i	fib	i

body	o	mop	o	toll	o
boat	o	mock	o	toad	o
bowl	o	mob	o	toe	o
bone	o	most	o	Tom	o

music	u	fruit	u	bug	u
mud	u	flute	u	bugle	u
mule	u	fun	u	bun	u
must	u	fume	u	bump	u

PHONICS PLAYGROUND

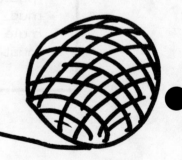

Game Activity

Directions:

1. Take all the cards from the box.

2. Sort the cards so that all the short vowels are together and all the long vowels are together.

3. Sort all the like sounds into stacks of words with a short a sound, short e sound, short i sound, etc.

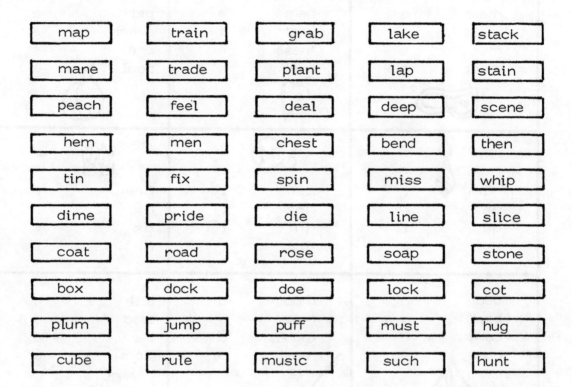

map	train	grab	lake	stack
mane	trade	plant	lap	stain
peach	feel	deal	deep	scene
hem	men	chest	bend	then
tin	fix	spin	miss	whip
dime	pride	die	line	slice
coat	road	rose	soap	stone
box	dock	doe	lock	cot
plum	jump	puff	must	hug
cube	rule	music	such	hunt

Draw two pictures, one that has a long vowel sound, one with a short vowel sound.

96

PHONICS PLAYGROUND

Find and circle all the words in this sentence which have the same vowel sound as <u>pie</u>.

1. Why is the sky filled with light on a night when there is no moonlight?

Find the words with the same vowel sound as <u>hat</u>

2. Pat can't work well at her center until she has her pencils, crayons, and tablet.

3. The fat man ran fast until he got tired and sat down under the apple tree.

Circle the words with the same vowel sound as <u>heat</u>.

4. I fell over my feet at the track meet and lost my keys to the jeep.

Circle the words with the same vowel sounds as <u>cup</u>.

5. A bee stung my thumb while I was eating lunch under the old tree.

6. Pug put his cupcake in the clubhouse that was up in the tree.

Circle the words with the same vowel sound as <u>hope</u>.

7. Smoke was floating from the closed oven door and the roast began to burn.

Write a sentence that has at least three long vowel sounds and two short vowel sounds.

PHONICS PLAYGROUND

Write each word under the letter that has the same vowel sound.

sock	huge	rose	peach	drop	
grape	check	snake	grin	zip	
scratch	toes	toes	trick	tie	hunt
tent	trap	bed	bus	rain	smoke
snail	pay	pie	prize	street	coat
block	lunch	while	roast	price	fuse
split	mule	strap	stump	cute	shine
wheel	grand	jeep	cup	feet	music
peg	stop	peck	trick	shock	

$$\bar{a} \quad \bar{e} \quad \bar{\imath} \quad \bar{o} \quad \bar{u}$$

$$\breve{a} \quad \breve{e} \quad \breve{\imath} \quad \breve{o} \quad \breve{u}$$

Add one of your own words to each square.

98

Rite - A - Report

PURPOSE:

After completing this center, the student should be able to use the encyclopedia as a resource tool to locate information necessary for writing a report.

MATERIALS:

Illustration and title
Encyclopedias
Pencils
Writing paper
Tagboard

List of ten explorers:

Byrd	Marco Polo
Columbus	John Glenn
Magellan	Lewis & Clark
Cortez	Ponce DeLeon
Perry	Leif Ericson

PROCEDURE:

1. Place all materials in the center, including the list of explorers printed on tagboard.

2. Introduce the center to enable the student to complete activities independently.

3. Provide time for evaluation of each completed activity and record individual student progress.

4. Make provision for filing or displaying completed activities.

RITE-A-REPORT

Select an explorer from the list that you would like to learn about.

1. Explorer's name _____

2. What year was he born? _____

3. Where was he born? _____

4. List three things he did when he was young.

   (1) _____

   (2) _____

   (3) _____

5. Where did he explore?

   _____

   _____

   _____

6. What means of transportation did he employ during his explorations?

   _____

   _____

7. What reasons did he have for making the trips? _____

   _____

   _____

8. List three outcomes of his explorations.

   _____

   _____

   _____

RITE-A-REPORT

Using the "Calling All Cats" activity sheet, develop an outline.

Explorer _____

I   Early Life

    A. _____

    B. _____

    C. _____

II   Explorations

    A. _____

    B. _____

    C. _____

III   Results of Explorations

    A. _____

    B. _____

    C. _____

Using a sheet of drawing paper, draw the means of transportation your explorer used.

RITE-A-REPORT

Write a report following the "Cool Cat" outline.

Explorer _____

_____

_____

_____

_____

_____

_____

_____

_____

_____

_____

_____

_____

_____

_____

Make a map showing the route of the exploration.

RITE-A-REPORT

Use the encyclopedia to develop an outline and write a
report about another explorer from the list. Use scratch
paper for your outline and discuss it with the teacher. Make
a rough draft of your report before writing the final report
here.

Explorer_____

_____

_____

_____

_____

_____

_____

_____

_____

_____

_____

_____

_____

_____

Read a book about this explorer and share it with the class.

Syllable Search

PURPOSE:

> After completing this center, the student should be able to identify and use syllables.

MATERIALS:

Illustration and title
Writing paper
Activity sheets
Tagboard cards
Game markers
Syllable Champ game
Tagboard

PROCEDURE:

1. Make "Syllable Flip Up" game and "Syllable Champ" game according to directions outlined on "Smarty Cat" and "Super Cat" activities.

2. Place all materials in the center.

3. Introduce the center to enable the student to complete activities independently.

4. Provide time for evaluation of each completed activity and record individual student progress.

5. Make provisions for filing or displaying completed activities.

SYLLABLE SEARCH

Write the number of vowels you hear in each word. In the next column write the number of syllables. In the last column write a new word with the same number of syllables.

	Vowel Sounds	Syllables	New Word
1. purple			
2. caterpillar			
3. folder			
4. zebra			
5. lemonade			
6. lollipop			
7. desk			
8. baseball			
9. chimpanzee			
10. sunshine			
11. boy			
12. piano			
13. cloudy			
14. simple			
15. happily			
16. sour			

SYLLABLE SEARCH

Say each word. Divide the word into syllables and write each syllable on the line.

always _____   leaf _____

squirrel _____   chipmunk _____

ladder _____   acorn _____

suddenly _____   behind _____

forever _____   wonderful _____

puppy _____   goat _____

country _____   handkerchief _____

picnic _____   shoe _____

earring _____   table _____

Complete this story by filling the 2-syllable words in the blanks.

1.   One day we went to the _____.

          lake   circus   store

2.   We _____ very early.

          left   walked   arrived

3.   Once there we bought our _____.

          tickets   dog   crackerjacks

4.   First we saw the _____.

          clowns   elephants   horses

5.   They were _____.

          tame   pretty   wild

Draw a picture of a part of the circus you would like to see.

106

SYLLABLE SEARCH

Directions for "Syllable Flip-Up" game.

1. Place the deck of word cards in a pile face down.

2. Give each player cards labeled with the words one syllable, two syllables, three syllables, and four syllables.

3. Direct one player to flip up a word card. Each player then holds up a card with the number of syllables they think is in the word.

4. The player holding up the correct cards scores one point.

5. The game continues for a specified time, and the player with the most points wins.

Words for the cards:

Monday	horseback	butterfly	understand	straight
pretty	rider	hospital	important	shivering
sad	automobile	emergency	drier	delightful
glad	picture	helpful	caged	bare
flower	alphabet	linoleum	narrow	alligator
poem	classroom	hippopotamus	easily	terrible
ranch	lawnmower	elephant	footprint	station
pencil	piano	ribbon	spends	lettuce
sandwich	whistle	people	puzzle	because
hero	warmest	watchful	smaller	weaker
graceful	scarf	mistake	correct	play
question	common	whole	rhymes	beginning

Write a sentence containing all one-syllable words. Now do one with all two-syllable words. Can you do a three-syllable-word sentence?

SYLLABLE SEARCH

Directions for "Syllable Champ" game:

1. Place the deck of word cards in a pile face down.

2. One at a time players draw a card and move one space for each syllable in the word. If the answer is incorrect, they move back two spaces.

3. The player to reach the Syllable Champ circle first wins.

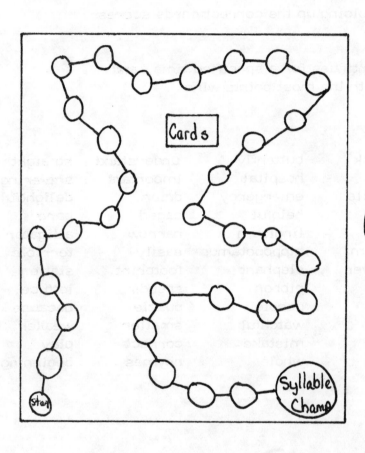

Use the words from the other game activity. Use a coin, washer or plastic marker for each player's man.

Shiv-er-ing I can move 3 spaces!

Choose fifteen word cards and in your tablet write each word and divide it into syllables.

The Big Lick

PURPOSE:
> After completing this center, the student should be able to express himself more creatively.

MATERIALS:
Illustration and title
Tagboard strips
Activity sheets

PROCEDURE:

1. Arrange center with illustration, title, activity sheets and ice cream cones with ideas for writing.

2. Introduce the center to enable the student to use it independently as often as he wishes.

3. Provide time for students to share completed stories in small groups.

4. Prepare a special bulletin board for displaying the completed "story cones".

THE BIG LICK

Enlarge these idea cones on tagboard and place in the center.

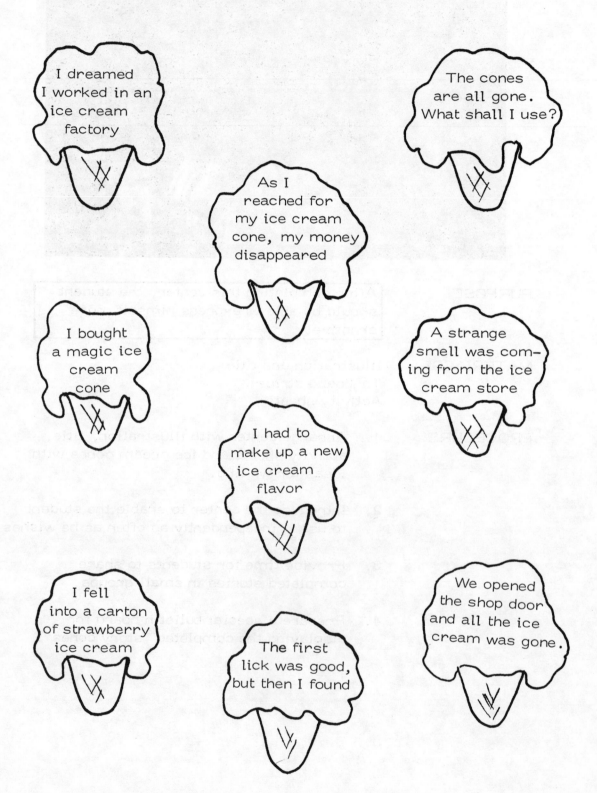

Tricky Fox

PURPOSE: | After completing this center, the student should be able to recognize the complete subject and the complete predicate in each sentence.

MATERIALS: Illustration and title
Directions
Activity sheets

PROCEDURE: 1.   Place all materials in center.

                    2.   Introduce center to enable the students to complete activities independently.

                    3.   Provide time for evaluation of each completed activity and record individual student progress.

                    4.   Make provision for filing or displaying completed activities.

TRICKY FOX

Draw one line under the complete subject, and two lines under the complete predicate in the following sentences.

1. Thirty children are in our class.

2. Mother made gingerbread for lunch.

3. We gathered leaves for our science project.

4. Our class is learning about space.

5. Jim and John had a Halloween party.

6. The policeman helped us cross the street.

7. Aunt Mary gave me a book for my birthday.

8. The museum was closed when we arrived.

9. Nancy got a bicycle for her birthday.

10. Kate and her mother watched the bees gather honey.

11. Mother, Daddy, and I pulled weeds in the garden.

12. My friends went deep sea fishing.

13. We watch television every night.

14. She went to the circus on Monday.

15. The school had a spaghetti supper.

subject + predicate = sentence !

TRICKY FOX

Underline the subject. List the nouns and the verbs in the appropriate columns.

		Nouns	Verbs
1.	The dew sparkled on the roses.	_____	_____
2.	Joe ran all the way to school.	_____	_____
3.	Some girls played ball with us.	_____	_____
4.	The river flowed gently by.	_____	_____
5.	Mary thanked him for the gift.	_____	_____
6.	The boy swam well in the meet.	_____	_____
7.	Birds fly south in winter.	_____	_____
8.	The boat sailed down the river.	_____	_____
9.	Mr. Jones hunts deer in the forest.	_____	_____
10.	Fir trees grow slowly near the Arctic Circle.	_____	_____
11.	Salmon swim upstream to lay their eggs.	_____	_____
12.	My mother is a third grade teacher.	_____	_____

Choose three subjects from the sentences above and write new sentences using different complete predicates.

TRICKY FOX

Write the simple subject of each sentence under the correct heading. Write the verb under the heading verb.

1. The pirates found the buried treasure.

2. She made a trip to see her aunt.

3. The apples were big and red.

4. No one came to visit me.

5. He built a tree house.

6. The boy caught his kite in the tree.

7. Our canoe tipped over.

8. I went camping in the state park.

9. Everyone had a great time at the party.

10. A circus came to our city.

11. They ate lunch with us.

12. Someone called me last night.

13. The clown marched in the parade.

14. Mrs. Jones is my neighbor.

15. We had a party at school.

Noun	Personal Pronoun	Indefinite Pronoun	Verb

Choose one sentence and write a paragraph about it.

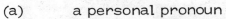

TRICKY FOX

Underline the subject of each sentence.
Tell whether the subject is:

    (a)   a personal pronoun
    (b)   a proper noun
    (c)   a common noun
    (d)   a determiner and a common noun

Example: The boy is in the third grade.   (d)

1.   Tom was hoeing corn in the garden. _____

2.   The dog followed Johnny to school. _____

3.   They had fun watching the monkeys at the zoo. _____

4.   The lion growled at the children. _____

5.   I like to feed the ducks at the park. _____

6.   Boys like to play football during physical education. _____

7.   Jane was eating candy before dinner. _____

8.   We are going on a field trip to the museum. _____

9.   The neighbors are having a party. _____

10.   Three kittens lost their mittens. _____

11.   Dogs like to chase rabbits. _____

12.   Dr. Johnson put my broken leg in a cast. _____

13.   She is sick today.

14.   A helicopter landed in the shopping center. _____

15.   He is a fast runner and won the race. _____

With a friend write five sentences. One will write a subject,
and the other a complete predicate. Put them together
to make fun sentences!

115

Witty Kitty

PURPOSE: After completing this center, the student should be able to write a letter correctly.

MATERIALS: Illustration and title
Activity sheets
Crayons
Ruler
Pencils
Tagboard

PROCEDURE: 1.   Place all materials in the center.

2.   Introduce the center to enable the student to complete activities independently.

3.   Provide time for evaluation of each completed activity and record individual student progress.

4.   Make provisions for filing or displaying completed activities.

WITTY KITTY

Write <u>yes</u> before each sentence that tells something that you should do when you write a letter. Write <u>no</u> before each incorrect sentence.

_____ 1. A period is used after each line in a letter.

_____ 2. The right margin is kept straight.

_____ 3. The date should go in the heading.

_____ 4. In the closing all words should be capitalized.

_____ 5. A comma goes between the city and state.

_____ 6. The signature is the name of the person who wrote the letter.

_____ 7. The date goes first in the heading.

_____ 8. The first word in the body of the letter should be indented.

_____ 9. A comma is used at the end of the greeting.

_____ 10. There are three commas in the heading.

_____ 11. A heading should be used when you write an invitation.

_____ 12. The return address on the envelope is in the upper right-hand corner.

_____ 13. Your zip code should be included in the heading.

_____ 14. The signature is the last part of the letter.

_____ 15. The name of a street should be capitalized.

_____ 16. Every letter has three main parts.

WITTY KITTY

Study the letter below so you know what the main parts of a letter are. Also check for punctuation and capital letters.

1. Heading – the address of   (21530 Main Street
       the person sending the letter   (Cleveland, Ohio 44135
                                                        (July 25, 1973

2. Greeting   (Dear Sue,

                        (We are having a lot of fun on our vacation.
                        (
                        (We went swimming yesterday and played
3. Body   (in the sand. Mother said we are going to the
                        (Aquarium this afternoon. I am anxious to see
                        (all the fish.
                        (
                        (We will be home Saturday.

4. Closing   (Your friend,

5. Signature   (Sally

The envelope should have two names and addresses on it.

person who   (Sally Wilson
wrote the   (21530 Main Street
letter   (Cleveland, Ohio 44135

person who   (Miss Sue Baker
is to receive   (4414 West Avenue
the letter   (Nashville, Tennessee 37204

WITTY KITTY

List the five parts of a letter. After each one write
an example.

1. _____   _____
                                          _____
                                          _____
                                          _____

2. _____
   _____

3. _____
   _____
   _____
   _____
   _____

4. _____   _____

5. _____   _____

Using your own address, write a heading.

WITTY KITTY

In two weeks you will have a birthday. Mother says
you can have a birthday party. Write a letter inviting
a friend to your birthday party.

_____

_____

_____

_____

_____

_____

_____

_____

_____

_____

_____

_____

                                    _____

Fold the invitation and design the outside cover.

WITTY KITTY

Your aunt has given you a gift for your birthday. Write
a letter thanking her for your gift.

_____

_____

_____

_____

_____

_____

_____

_____

_____

_____

_____

_____

_____

_____

_____

_____

_____

_____

_____

At the bottom of the letter draw a picture of the
gift your aunt gave you.

WITTY KITTY

Write a letter to a friend you haven't seen in a long time. Place the heading, greeting, body, closing and signature correctly. Proofread your letter to make sure you have the correct punctuation.

_____

_____

_____

_____

_____

_____

_____

_____

_____

_____

_____

_____

_____

_____

_____

_____

On the back of the letter, draw an envelope three inches by six inches. Address the envelope correctly and design a stamp.

Environmental Centers

Notes.

All About Me!

PURPOSE:

After completing this center, the student should be more aware of his own individuality and be more sensitive to his own and other people's emotions.

MATERIALS:

Illustration and title
Activity sheets
Drawing paper, pencils, crayons
Magazines

PROCEDURE:

1. Cut pictures of people showing different emotions from magazines. Number and display them, following directions given in "Super Cat" activity.

2. Place all materials in the center.

3. Provide time for evaluation of each completed activity and record individual student progress.

4. Make provision for filing or displaying completed activities.

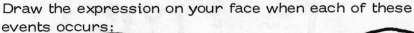

ALL ABOUT ME

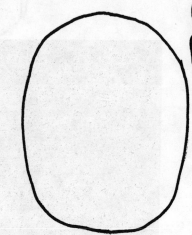

Draw the expression on your face when each of these events occurs:

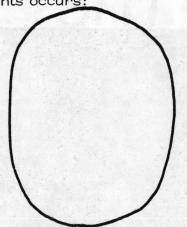

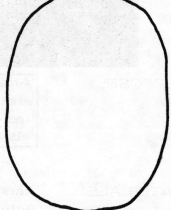

1. A babysitter is coming.

2. My puppy is lost.

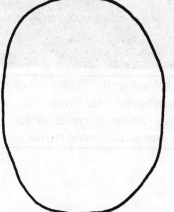

3. I have opened a present I love!

4. I have been punished.

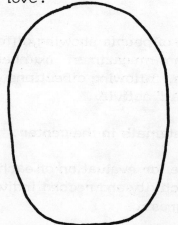

5. We are having cauliflower for dinner.

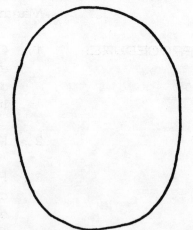

6. I haven't completed my schoolwork.

ALL ABOUT ME

Everyone has favorite people, places, or things.
Describe your favorites below.

1. My favorite friend is _____ because

   _____

2. My favorite T. V. program is _____ because

   _____

3. My favorite food is _____ because

   _____

4. My favorite sport is _____ because

   _____

5. My favorite book is _____ because

   _____

6. My favorite song is _____ because

   _____

7. My favorite movie was _____ because

   _____

8. My favorite vacation place is _____ because

   _____

9. My favorite color is _____ because

   _____

10. My favorite animal is _____ because

   _____

Draw a picture of one of your favorite things and ask two
friends to guess what it is.

ALL ABOUT ME

Hostility sometimes occurs when a person is against
or opposed to something. People may get angry or mad.
Lots of people or things can cause us to feel hostility.

When I'm at home:

    My mother makes me angry when she

    _____

    My father makes me angry when he

    _____

When I'm playing:

    My friends make me angry when _____

    _____

When I'm at school:

    My teacher makes me angry when _____

    _____

    A student makes me angry when _____

    _____

When I'm alone:

    I make myself angry when _____

    _____

Others can tell when I am angry because I

_____

Is it good to be angry at times? Write a short paragraph,
poem, or story expressing your feelings about anger.

128

ALL ABOUT ME

Study the pictures that are on the board of people showing different emotions. All these pictures show certain kinds of feelings. Match the number below with the number of the picture and write the emotion you think is being expressed and why.

	Emotion?	Why?
1.	_____	_____
2.	_____	_____
3.	_____	_____
4.	_____	_____
5.	_____	_____
6.	_____	_____
7.	_____	_____
8.	_____	_____
9.	_____	_____
10.	_____	_____
11.	_____	_____
12.	_____	_____
13.	_____	_____
14.	_____	_____
15.	_____	_____

Look through the magazines to find a picture that shows frustration, one that shows disbelief, and one that shows pleasure. Mount them on a piece of construction paper and label them.

PURPOSE: After completing this center, the student
                should be able to identify the planets in our
                solar system and be familiar with some of
                their properties.

MATERIALS: Illustration and title
                Encyclopedias, resource books
                Activity sheets
                Construction paper
                Dice, crayons

PROCEDURE: 1. Make the Space Race Game and include
                    optional activity directions. Print words
                    found in "Cool Cat" activity on strips of
                    tagboard and place in Blast Off capsule,
                    made by covering a paper towel tube to
                    look like a capsule.

                2. Place all materials in the center.

                3. Discuss the center concept and explain the
                    activities to enable the student to complete
                    activities independently.

                4. Provide time for evaluation of each completed
                    activity and record individual student progress.

                5. Make provision for filing or displaying
                    completed activities.

BLAST OFF

Use a resource book to complete these sentences.

1. A solar system is _____

    _____

2. The planets in our solar system are _____

    _____

    _____

3. We live on planet _____.

4. The smallest planet is _____.

5. The planet that is always covered with clouds is _____.

6. The red planet is _____.

7. The largest planet is _____.

8. One planet that has rings around it is _____.

9. The planet that is furthest away from earth is _____.

10. Which planet would you most like to visit? _____.

    Why? _____

    _____

    _____

    _____

    _____

BLAST OFF

Words to be used with crossword puzzles.

elevator	parachute	
launch	astronaut	Mercury
lift off	helmet	earth
moon	lox	Pluto
Canaveral	rotate	space suit
Neptune	Venus	carrier
Uranus	Jupiter	hangar
Mars	Saturn	heat shield
countdown		capsule

BLAST OFF

Use the clues below to fill in the blanks. The words in the
Blast Off capsule will help you.

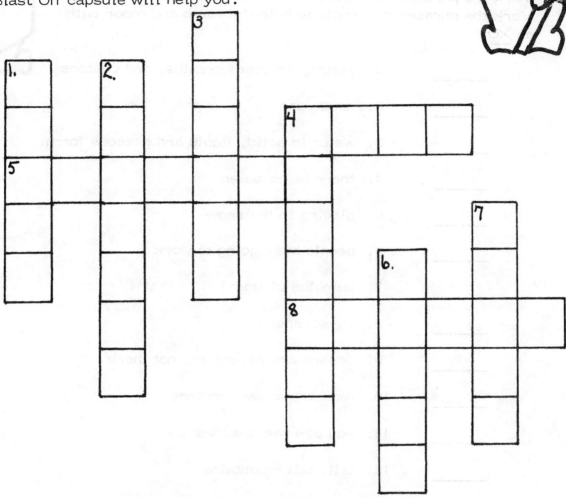

Down:
1. A planet always covered by clouds is _____ .
2. A large red spot is found on _____ .
3. _____ has large rings circling it.
4. The planet nearest the sun is _____ .
6. People live on _____ .
7. The planet furthest from the sun is _____ .

Across:
4. The red planet is called _____ .
5. _____ and Uranus are often called the
twin planets.
8. Very little is known about _____ .

Draw each planet and the sun as you think they look in space.
Cut them out and mount them in order on blue paper.

BLAST OFF

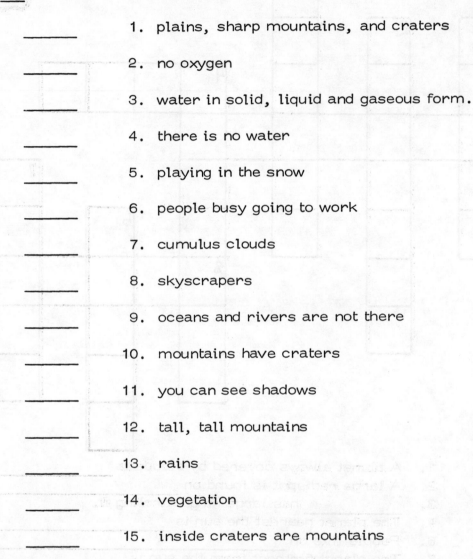

Mark the phrases that apply to the earth with an X.
Mark the phrases that apply to the moon with an O.
Mark the phrases that apply to both the earth and moon with an XO.

_____ 1. plains, sharp mountains, and craters

_____ 2. no oxygen

_____ 3. water in solid, liquid and gaseous form.

_____ 4. there is no water

_____ 5. playing in the snow

_____ 6. people busy going to work

_____ 7. cumulus clouds

_____ 8. skyscrapers

_____ 9. oceans and rivers are not there

_____ 10. mountains have craters

_____ 11. you can see shadows

_____ 12. tall, tall mountains

_____ 13. rains

_____ 14. vegetation

_____ 15. inside craters are mountains

Discuss this activity with a friend. Pretend you are astronauts looking at the moon for the first time.

BLAST OFF

These are the clues for the crossword puzzle. The words in the Blast Off capsule will help you.

Across:

1. The upward movement as the rocket takes off

3. The calling out the seconds just before the firing of the rocket

5. A planet that we may explore next

7. Person who travels on a space ship

9. A machine that takes the astronauts up to the capsule

11. A ship with a large deck that planes can land on

13. Strong covering on the capsule that protects it from heat

Down:

2. A building for planes

4. To begin the ship upward

6. A shortened name for liquid oxygen

8. A suit worn to protect the astronaut

10. Part of the rocket the astronauts travel in

12. Most rockets are launched at Cape Kennedy, once named Cape _____.

14. An object that helps to slow down the capsule so it can land.

16. The earth's satellite is called a _____.

18. Worn on the astronaut's head

20. _____ means to spin on its axis.

BLAST OFF

BLAST OFF

Space Race Game:
(for two or more players)

Directions:

1. Roll the dice to see who begins. High number starts.
2. Begin with one die; each player gets one roll of the die.
3. You must move in order. Only after you roll a 1 can you do the activity for No. 1; then you must roll a 2 to do the next activity.
4. Once you have completed the 6th activity, roll two dice.
5. The first player to travel all through space and complete the activities wins.

Roll:

1   Color the sun.

2   This is the smallest planet; label it.

3   Venus is always covered with clouds; label it and color it.

4   Color the earth and label it.

5   Draw a moon revolving around earth.

6   Mars is known as the red planet; color it to show that.

7   This is the largest planet; label it and mark the red spot on it.

8   Color the rings around Saturn and label it.

9   Label Uranus and color it.

10   Neptune is very similar to Uranus; color it the same.

11   Label the planet that is the furthest from the sun and color it.

12   Color your space ship – you've won!

138

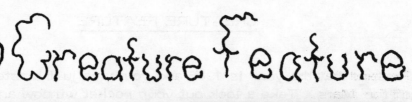

Creature Feature

PURPOSE:

After completing this center, the student should be able to think creatively about space.

MATERIALS:

Illustration and title
Activity sheets
Encyclopedias
Crayons, string, construction paper
Hangers for mobile
Paint

PROCEDURE:

1. Place all materials in the center.

2. Verbally introduce the center to enable the student to complete activities independently.

3. Provide time for evaluation of each completed activity and record individual student progress.

4. Arrange "Space Place" corner or bulletin board and make provisions for filing or displaying all completed activities.

139

CREATURE FEATURE

Pretend that the year is 1986 and you have just blasted off for Mars. Take a look out your rocket window and draw a picture of six things you see in space. Be sure to label and color each picture.

1. _____	2. _____
3. _____	4. _____
5. _____	6. _____

CREATURE FEATURE

You have been employed by the space center to design
a new space ship to blast off in the year 1986.

The inside of the space ship needs designing too!

Make a list of supplies you will need to put aboard before
you blast off.

CREATURE FEATURE

Use your imagination to complete this story.

The spaceship Cosmocraft streaked toward the
hazy planet. Finally the spacemen had reached
their destination. As they landed, a strange green
mist was forming. The mist turned into the form
of a creature. What should they do? The earliest
possible takeoff time would be three and one-half
hours away.

_____

_____

_____

_____

_____

_____

_____

_____

_____

_____

_____

_____

Illustrate your story by drawing and coloring <u>very lightly</u>
over the story.

142

CREATURE FEATURE

This boy will be the first boy in space. Design a space
suit for him. Draw it on top of him and label all the
different parts.

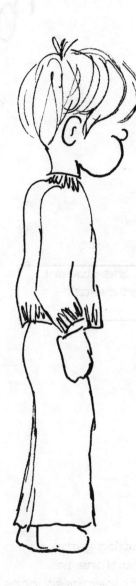
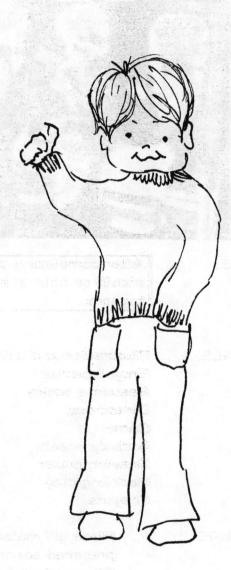

Why is it necessary to wear space suits? _____

_____

Using a resource book, write a paragraph telling about space
suits and why they are worn by astronauts.

Don't Lose Your Choppers

PURPOSE: After completing this center, the student
             should be able to practice good dental
             hygiene.

MATERIALS: Illustration and title
             Encyclopedias
             Resource books
             Directions
             Game
             Activity sheets
             Drawing paper
             Modeling clay
             Crayons

PROCEDURE: 1. Place all materials, including game
                 prepared according to directions in
                 "Super Cat" activity, and other resources
                 in the center.

             2. Introduce the center to enable the student
                 to complete activities independently.

             3. Provide time for evaluation of each com-
                 plated activity and record individual student
                 progress. Make provision for filing or
                 displaying completed activities.

144

DON'T LOSE YOUR CHOPPERS

Use a resource book of your own selection to find the following information.

1. The two sets of teeth are _____

   and _____ .

2. How many teeth are in each set? _____

3. Name the three parts of a tooth. _____ ,

   _____ , and _____

4. Name the kinds of teeth and tell what each kind does. _____

   _____

   _____

5. Define the crown and root of the tooth. _____

   _____

6. What food is good for building strong teeth? _____

7. Name three ways to take care of your teeth.

   (1) _____

   (2) _____

   (3) _____

8. What causes a cavity? _____

   _____

9. Name three ways teeth help you. (1) _____

   (2) _____ (3) _____

10. What is flouride and how does it help? _____

    _____

DON'T LOSE YOUR CHOPPERS

Write a good dental health rule. Now draw a picture
in the frame below to illustrate your rule. When you
are satisfied with your picture, go to the art center
and get materials to make a poster.

Enter your poster in the "Poster Parade" by pinning it
on the "Poster Parade" board.

DON'T LOSE YOUR CHOPPERS

Draw a tooth 8 inches long. Show each part of the tooth
by making a cross section of it. Color the tooth and
label all the different parts. Use the resource books in
the center to help you.

Go to the art center and make a model of the tooth from
clay.

DON'T LOSE YOUR CHOPPERS

Game Activity:

1.   List each question on a tagboard card shaped as
      a toothbrush.

2.   Object is to brush every tooth first.

3.   Make dial with spinner. As child answers question correctly,
      he can move the number of spaces he spins.

Questions:

1.   How many sets of teeth will you have?

2.   Name the two sets of teeth.

3.   How many teeth are in the primary set?

4.   How many in the permanent set?

5.   Name two ways to take care of your teeth.

6.   Name the three parts of a tooth.

7.   What is the outside of a tooth called?

8.   What is the soft part of a tooth called?

9.   What is the best food for building good teeth?

10.   How many times should you visit the dentist each year?

11.   Why is it important to visit the dentist?

12.   How does dental floss help?

13.   Name two ways your teeth help you.

14.   What teeth are called the grinders?

15.   What teeth tear your food?

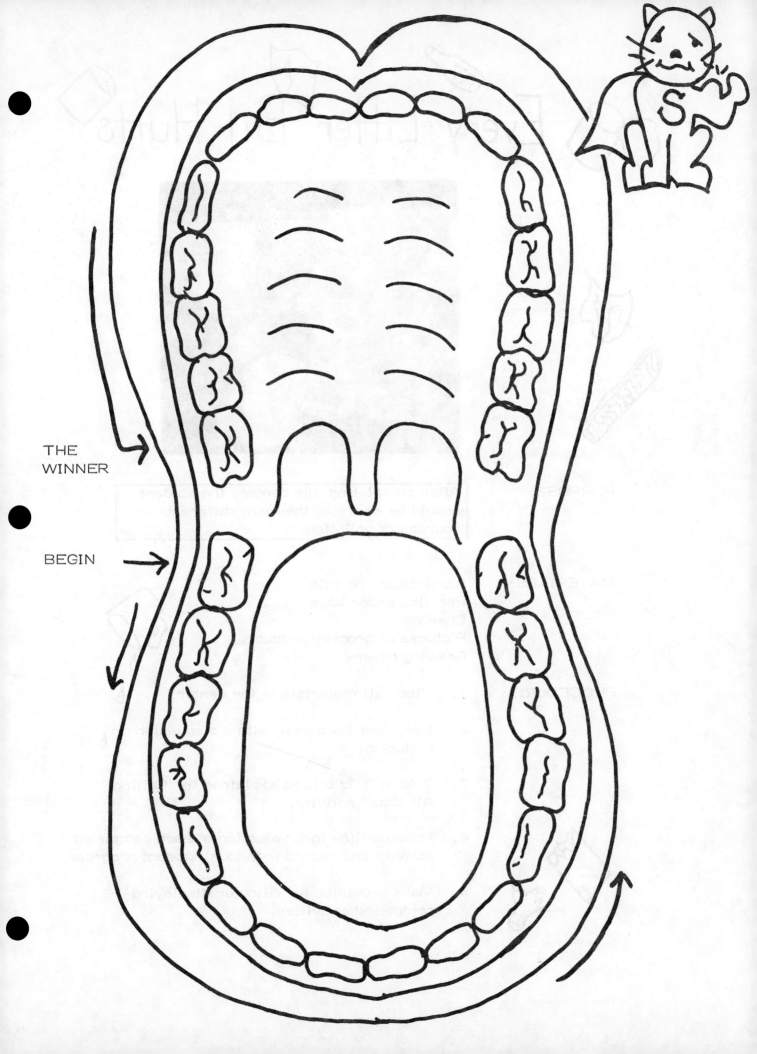

THE
WINNER

BEGIN

Every Litter Bit Hurts

PURPOSE:

> After completing this center, the student should be aware of the many different sources of pollution.

MATERIALS:
Illustration and title
Pencils, paper bags
Crayons
Pictures of grocery products
Drawing paper

PROCEDURE:

1. Place all materials in the center.

2. Introduce the center with a discussion on pollution.

3. Take a field trip as explained in "Calling All Cats" activity.

4. Provide time for evaluation of each completed activity and record individual student progress.

5. Make provision for filing or displaying completed activities.

EVERY LITTER BIT HURTS

To introduce this center, take the entire class on a walking field trip around the campus or the surrounding neighborhood. After a general discussion concerning pollution, provide each student with a paper bag to contain litter collected during the walk.

After completing the field trip, ask the students to examine and classify the litter to make a composite chart. While students are working in the center, the chart can be analyzed and findings recorded.

Items found	Number of items found	Where items found	Guilty Persons	Solution

EVERY LITTER BIT HURTS

Using information from the chart, make a graph
showing the findings of the field trip. Use different
colored crayons to graph the results.

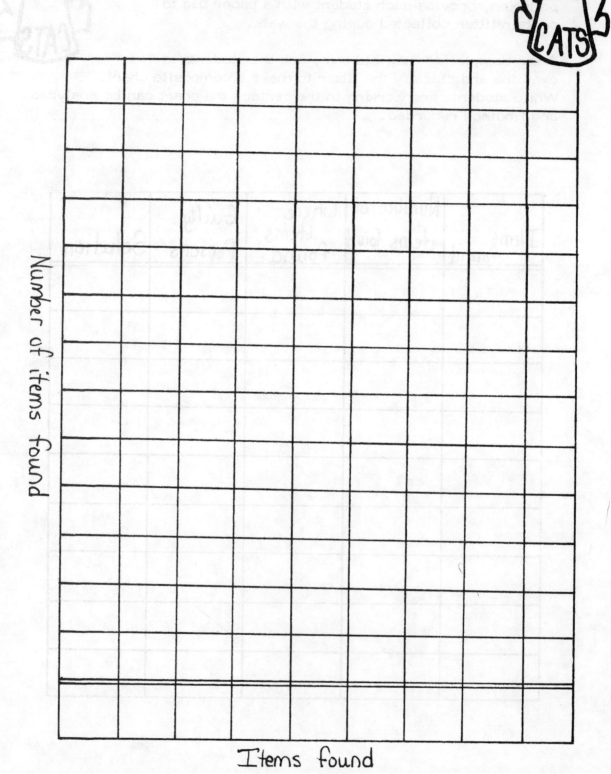

Number of items found

Items found

EVERY LITTER BIT HURTS

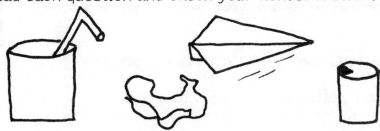

Read each question and check your honest answer.

		Yes	No
1.	Do you leave the water running when you brush your teeth?		
2.	Do you use paper cups and plates?		
3.	Do you drink milk with a straw?		
4.	Do you use colored Kleenex?		
5.	Do you use just one side of your writing paper?		
6.	Do you make one mistake and throw your paper away?		
7.	Do you use scraps of art materials?		
8.	Do you see papers on the floor and leave them?		
9.	Do you ever write on walls, books, floors or bulletin boards?		
10.	Do you break plastic spoons so they can't be reused?		
11.	Do you drink pop from cans?		
12.	Do you use two paper towels rather than one?		
13.	Have you ever thrown anything out a car window?		
14.	Do you waste paper to make paper airplanes?		
15.	Have you ever broken a branch off a tree?		
16.	Do you throw away a pencil that could still be used?		

If you have more than five "yeses", you are guilty of polluting the earth.

List five things you could do to promote ecology.

153

EVERY LITTER BIT HURTS

There are many reasons for pollution. Choose one of these ideas or use an idea of your own and write a story about it.

    (1) Air pollution   (3) Noise pollution

    (2) Water pollution   (4) Litterbugs

Include in your story:

What causes this kind of pollution? Where does it happen? Who causes it? How can we solve this problem?

_____

_____

_____

_____

_____

_____

_____

_____

_____

_____

_____

_____

Draw a picture showing how you could solve the problem you have written about.

EVERY LITTER BIT HURTS

We have many great inventions, but some of them help cause air, water, or noise pollution. Make a list of great inventions and tell why they are <u>harmful</u> or <u>harmless</u> to pollution.

Invention	Why They are Harmful or Harmless to Pollution

Invent a machine that will help solve our pollution problems. Draw a picture of your invention and color it. Use the back of this activity sheet for your picture.

EVERY LITTER BIT HURTS

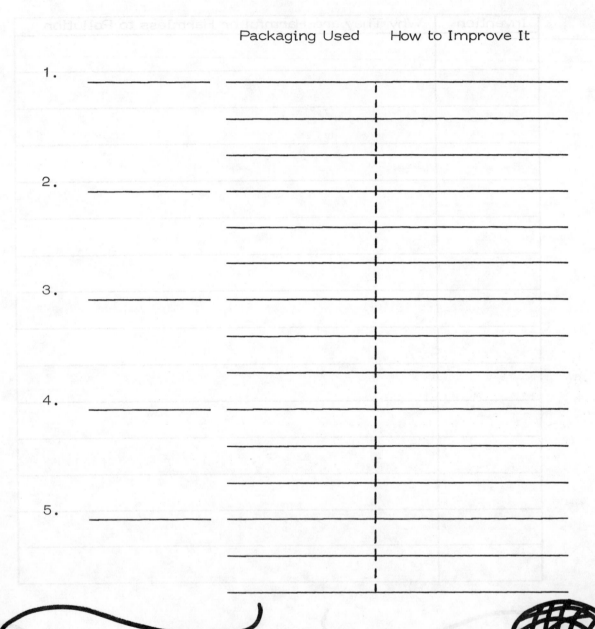

Look at the pictures of the grocery products. Many products have excess packaging that contributes to the waste problem.

How could these products be sold to lessen the amount of packaging?

	Packaging Used	How to Improve It
1.		
2.		
3.		
4.		
5.		

Go to the grocery store and count the number of grocery bags used in thirty minutes. Report this to the class with a suggested solution to this wastefulness.

Future Shock

PURPOSE: After completing this center, the student
            should be aware of his goals and ambitions
            for the future.

MATERIALS: Illustration and title
            Drawing paper, crayons
            Word die
            Construction paper, paste

PROCEDURE: 1. Make Word Dice according to directions
                given in "Smarty Cat" activity.

            2. Place all materials in the center.

            3. Introduce the center to enable the
                student to complete activities independently.

            4. Provide time for evaluation of each
                completed activity and record individual
                student progress.

            5. Make provision for filing or displaying
                completed activities.

FUTURE SHOCK

What will you look like in twenty years? How old will you be in twenty years? _____

Think about what your size will be, your clothes, your hair, and if your face will change at all.

Draw a picture of yourself as you think you will look in twenty years.

FUTURE SHOCK

Twenty years from now, where would you like to live?

_____

_____

Why would you want to live there? _____

_____

Below draw a picture of the type of home you would like to live in twenty years from now. Add the background.

Draw your favorite room in this home. Explain why it is your favorite room.

FUTURE SHOCK

Word Die — Take a square box and cover it with paper. From a magazine cut out words that are adjectives and adverbs and make a collage with the words and box.

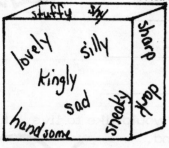

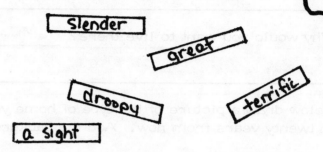

Roll the die. Look at the words on the die and put them into the appropriate columns. Roll the die as many times as you wish.

how I will look	how I will feel	how I will sound

Use a piece of construction paper and a magazine to make your own collage of words that describes yourself twenty years from now.

FUTURE SHOCK

As an adult twenty years from now you will have a job.
Write your job description and the qualifications for it.

_____

_____

_____

_____

_____

_____

_____

_____

_____

_____

_____

_____

_____

_____

_____

_____

Where do you work? What type of transportation do you
use to get to work? Write a story or draw a picture
describing either or both.

FUTURE SHOCK

Make a daily schedule for your future life style.
Include your working hours, meals, leisure time,
meetings, and any other activities.

Sunday	Monday	Tuesday
am. p.m.	a.m. p.m.	a.m. p.m.
Wednesday	**Thursday**	**Friday**
am. pm	am. pm.	a.m. p.m.

Saturday
am.   p.m.

Draw a picture of the family you would like to have.

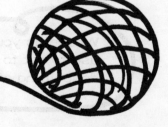

 # I ate the whole thing

PURPOSE: After completing this center, the student should be able to be more aware of good nutrition and develop better eating habits.

MATERIALS: Illustration and title
Scissors
Activity sheets
Pictures of fruits and vegetables
Encyclopedias
Basic food groups chart
Food Fair Box

PROCEDURE: 1. Place all materials in the center. Make Food Fair Box by cutting pictures of fruits and vegetables from a seed catalog and mounting them on 3" x 5" index cards. Place these on a box.

2. Introduce the center to enable the student to complete activities independently.

3. Provide time for evaluation of each completed activity and record individual progress.

4. Make provisions for filing or displaying completed activities.

I ATE THE WHOLE THING

Using the resource book, identify the four basic food groups and list them on the chart below. Draw six examples of foods belonging in each of the basic food groups.

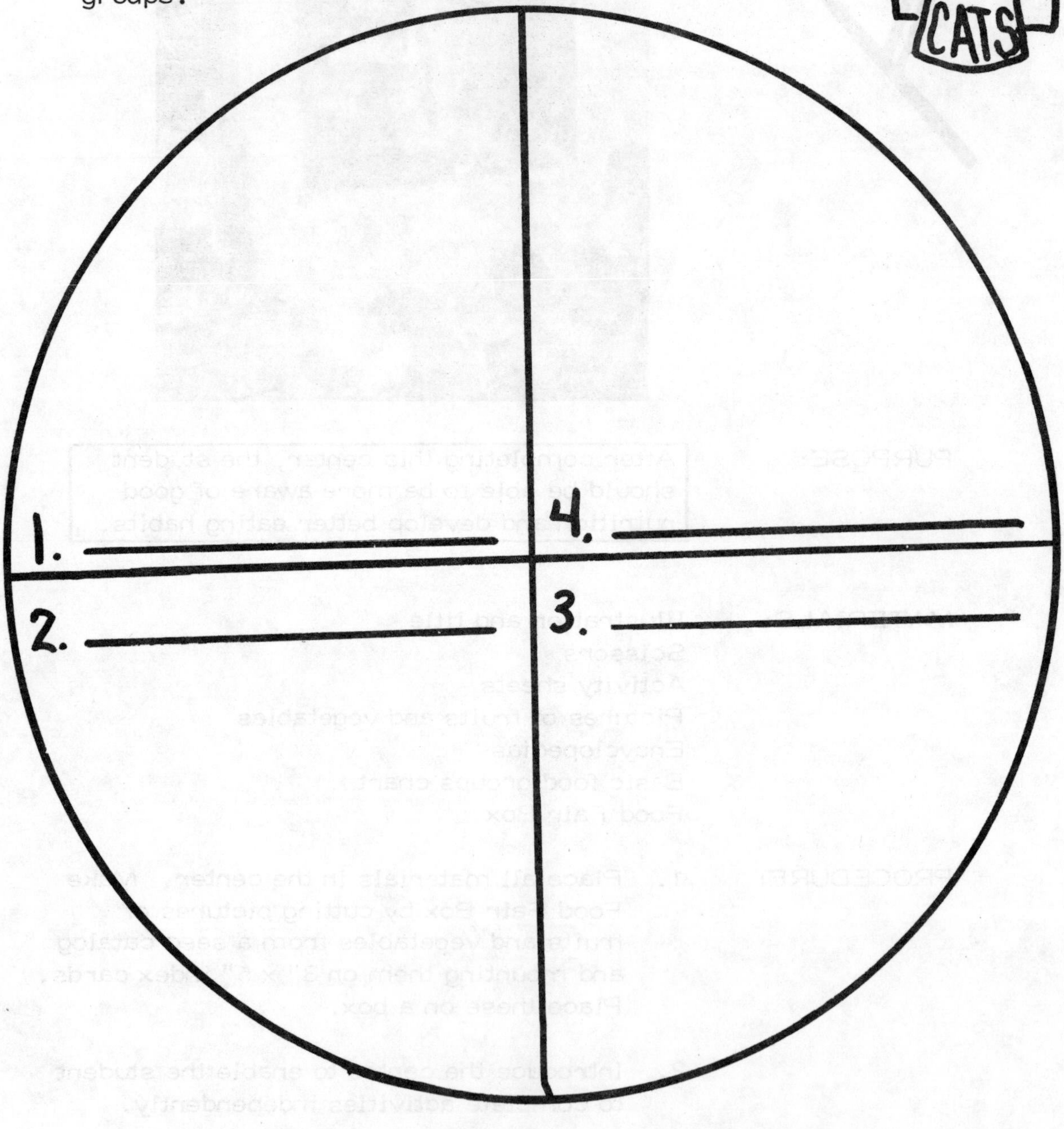

1. _____   4. _____

2. _____   3. _____

Use the resource book again to find out how many servings of each group we need to eat each day.

1. _____   3. _____

2. _____   4. _____

I ATE THE WHOLE THING

Use your "Calling All Cats" activity sheet to help you complete this activity. Plan a menu for two days to meet the daily requirements of the four food groups.

Day I

Breakfast:

Lunch:

Dinner:

Day II

Breakfast:

Lunch:

Dinner:

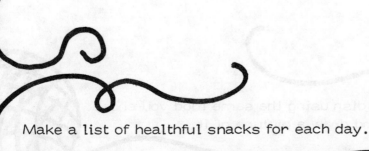

Make a list of healthful snacks for each day.

I ATE THE WHOLE THING

Choose one picture from the Food Fair Box. Think of as
many ways to serve this food as you can. Draw the
pictures showing them ready to be eaten. Label your
pictures and color them.

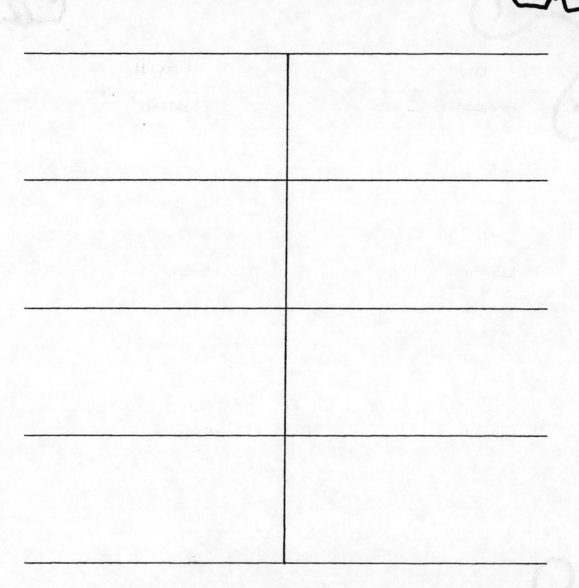

Make up your own dish using the same food you chose.
Write the recipe and draw a picture of it.

I ATE THE WHOLE THING

Many necessary preparations are made for food on the way from the grower to the table. Think of all the people responsible for the food you eat every day. Choose a food and write a paragraph telling about it from seed to table.

_____

_____

_____

_____

_____

_____

_____

_____

_____

_____

_____

_____

_____

_____

_____

Draw a picture showing all the different stages this food must go through before it reaches the table.

Land Ahoy

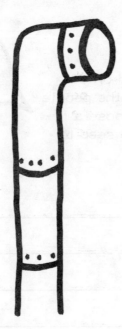

PURPOSE: | After completing this center, the student should be able to think creatively about adapting to a given situation.

MATERIALS: Illustration and title
Writing paper
Pencils
Gallon jug
Drawing paper
Crayons

PROCEDURE:

1. Place illustration, title, activity sheets, student materials and directions in the center.

2. Verbally introduce the center activities.

3. Provide time for evaluation of each completed activity and record individual student progress.

4. Make provision for filing or displaying completed activities.

LAND AHOY

Tell about the imaginary shipwreck you were in and how you managed to get to this island. Be sure to tell how many people were shipwrecked with you, what you were doing on the ship, where you had planned to go, and how the ship was wrecked. Tell how you escaped, how you got to this island, and how long it took for all of this to happen.

_____

_____

_____

_____

_____

_____

_____

_____

_____

_____

_____

_____

_____

_____

LAND AHOY

Since the shipwreck, many things have happened. Begin a diary telling about your adventures. The first day is the day you found the island.

Day of _____

_____

_____

_____

Day of _____

_____

_____

_____

Day of _____

_____

_____

_____

Day of _____

_____

_____

_____

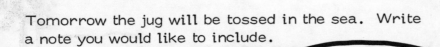

Tomorrow the jug will be tossed in the sea. Write a note you would like to include.

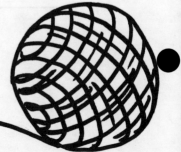

LAND AHOY

One of the first things needed on this island is some type of shelter. There are no close caves, and you have no tools or nails. What materials could you use to build your shelter?

Materials: _____

_____

_____

Draw a picture of the outside of your new home.

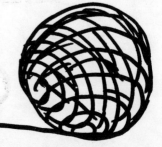

Show the inside of your home with a drawing. Include furniture if you have any and label the materials used.

LAND AHOY

The food you have found on this island is very different
from any food you know. Draw a picture of each food
found and describe its flavor, texture, and how it grows.

_____ | _____

_____

_____

_____

_____

_____

_____

_____

Make a sample menu using the foods.

172

LAND AHOY

Anywhere you live, there are dangers. Think of ten dangers that could be found on this island. List the ways you might protect yourself from these dangers.

Dangers	Ways to Protect Yourself
1.	
2.	
3.	
4.	
5.	
6.	
7.	
8.	
9.	
10.	

List twelve things you could do for fun on the island.

LAND AHOY

The survivors have asked you to survey the island and mark all the physical features. This will be useful if more food or water is needed, or if there is need to build new homes.

Draw an outline of the way the island looks, marking mountains, lakes, rivers, and any special vegetation. Include anything else that you feel is important. Name the landmarks on the map.

What would you name the island? _____
Design a flag for the island.

LAND AHOY

You have just been elected leader of the island. It
will be your responsibility to see that the other people
have food and shelter, and can live together peacefully.
Every person must assume his share of the responsibility.

Jobs Needed	Laws of the Island
1.	1.
2.	2.
3.	3.
4.	4.
5.	5.
6.	6.
7.	7.
8.	8.
9.	9.
10.	10.
11.	11.
12.	12.
13.	13.
14.	14.
15.	15.
16.	16.

Write a paragraph telling what you will do if a person
is lazy and won't do his job, or if someone breaks a law.

Mighty Magnets

PURPOSE:

> After completing this center, the student should be able to recognize the attractive properties of magnets.

MATERIALS:
Illustration and title
Activity sheets
Bar and horseshoe magnets of varying strengths
Box of objects including paper clips, brass
 fasteners, pins, ruler, nails, eraser, bottle
 caps, tacks, scissors
Piece of plastic
Tin can, glass jar, block of wood
Iron filings
Container of water, lightweight paper, sample of cloth

PROCEDURE:

1. Glue picture in box according to directions given in "Calling All Cats" activity.

2. Place all materials in the center.

3. Introduce the center to enable the student to complete activities independently.

4. Provide time for evaluation of each completed activity and record individual student progress.

5. Make provision for filing or displaying completed activities.

MIGHTY MAGNETS

Use the box of objects to help you decide what a magnet
will attract and repel. Draw and label each one.

A magnet will attract these 5 things:	A magnet will repel these 5 things:
1.	1.
2.	2.
3.	3.
4.	4.
5.	5.

Draw and label 2 additional objects that will attract a
magnet, and 2 additional objects that will repel a magnet.

MIGHTY MAGNETS

Teachers: Glue this picture of "Magnet Man" in the
bottom of a box. Place the iron filings on the
picture and use a magnet to attract the metal
filings through the cardboard.

Please give "Magnet Man" some hair! Move the magnet along
the bottom of the box pulling the iron filings. Move the iron
filings to give him hair on his head and perhaps even a beard or
moustache!

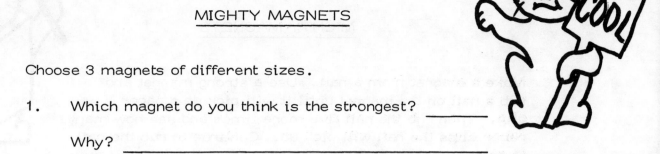

MIGHTY MAGNETS

Choose 3 magnets of different sizes.

1.   Which magnet do you think is the strongest? _____

     Why? _____

2.   Label each magnet A, B, or C. Using pins, test to
     see which attracts the largest number of pins. Fill
     in the graph.

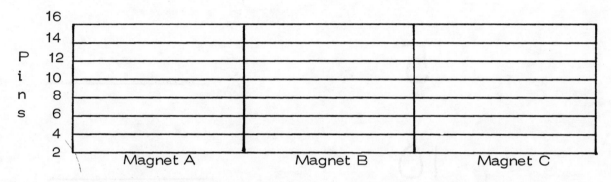

3.   The test above showed magnet _____ was the strongest.
     Did you guess correctly? _____

4.   Choose a horseshoe magnet. Draw on the magnet the number of
     pins each end will attract and the number of pins the middle will
     attract.

     The strongest part
     of a magnet is the

     _____

     _____.

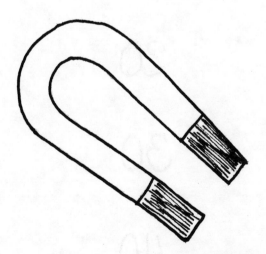

Using a bar magnet, test to find its strongest section.

179

MIGHTY MAGNETS

Make a magnet from a nail. Use a strong magnet and
rub a nail on the magnet until it will pick up a paper
clip. Then rub the nail five more times and see how many
paper clips the nail will pick up. Continue to rub the nail
to determine how many more paper clips the nail will pick
up. Record it on the chart below.

Number of times nail is rubbed: Number of paper clips picked up:

5   _____

10   _____

15   _____

20   _____

30   _____

40   _____

Experiment with 3 additional metal objects. Rub them on
a strong magnet to determine if they will attract other
metal objects.

MIGHTY MAGNETS

Use one magnet to test the strength of magnets through various substances.

List the number of pins this magnet can attract.

Test to see if the materials listed below will interfere with the magnets' attraction. Fill in the chart.

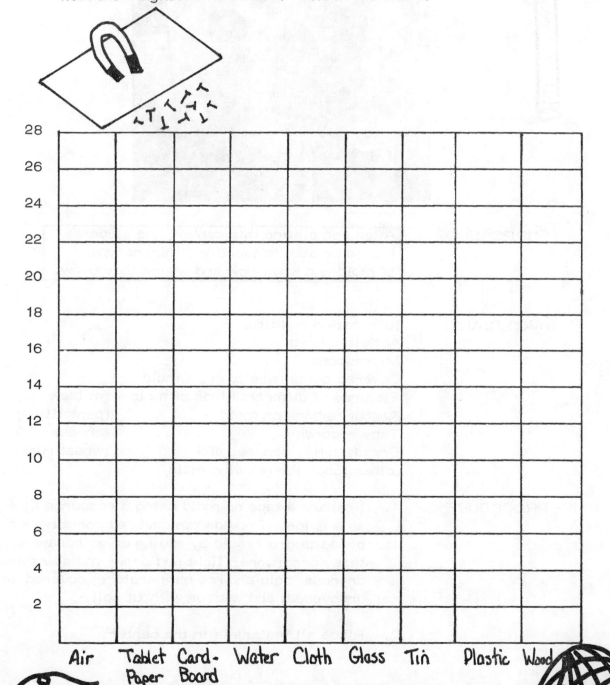

	Air	Tablet Paper	Card-Board	Water	Cloth	Glass	Tin	Plastic	Wood
28									
26									
24									
22									
20									
18									
16									
14									
12									
10									
8									
6									
4									
2									

Ends of magnets attract and others repel each other. Use two bar magnets to discover why this happens.

181

PURPOSE: After completing this center, the student
should be able to identify different types
of mold and know how and where they grow.

MATERIALS: Illustration and title
Activity sheets
Microscope
Covered containers to grow mold
Pictures of different kinds of mold – (mildew   )
Resource book on mold   (penicillin)
Tape recorder   (cheese   )
Bread, jelly, orange, and   (wheat rust)
  other foods for growing mold

PROCEDURE: 1. Prepare a tape on mold using a resource book
as a guide. Provide ten covered containers of
bread to grow mold by adding or withdrawing
these conditions: light and dark; moisture and
dryness; cold and hot temperature; covered or
uncovered; and with or without soil.

2. Place all materials in the center.

MOLDY OLDY

PROCEDURE: 3. Introduce the center to enable the student
                   to complete activities independently.

               4. Provide time for evaluation of each
                   completed activity and record individual
                   student progress including a daily
                   observation record of a mold colony.

               5. Make provisions for filing or displaying
                   completed activities.

add water

cover

with sun

use heat

with dirt

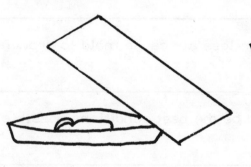

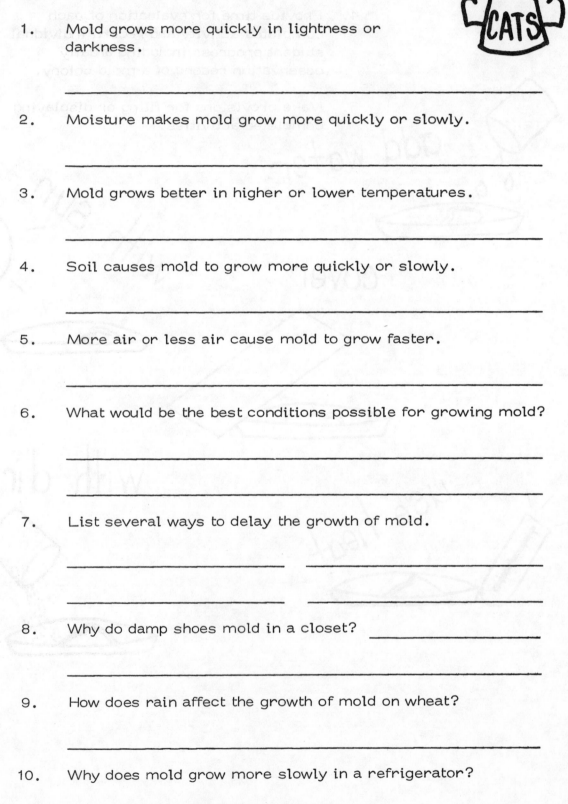

MOLDY OLDY

Study the ten containers of bread mold and the conditions that provided growth for each. Make these observations:

1. Mold grows more quickly in lightness or darkness.

    _____

2. Moisture makes mold grow more quickly or slowly.

    _____

3. Mold grows better in higher or lower temperatures.

    _____

4. Soil causes mold to grow more quickly or slowly.

    _____

5. More air or less air cause mold to grow faster.

    _____

6. What would be the best conditions possible for growing mold?

    _____

    _____

7. List several ways to delay the growth of mold.

    _____   _____

    _____   _____

8. Why do damp shoes mold in a closet? _____

    _____

9. How does rain affect the growth of mold on wheat?

    _____

10. Why does mold grow more slowly in a refrigerator?

    _____

MOLDY OLDY

Look at the mold on the bread. Write and describe how
it looks through the microscope. Tell about its shape,
size and its color.

At the bottom of the page draw a picture of what the bread
mold looks like.

_____

_____

_____

_____

_____

_____

_____

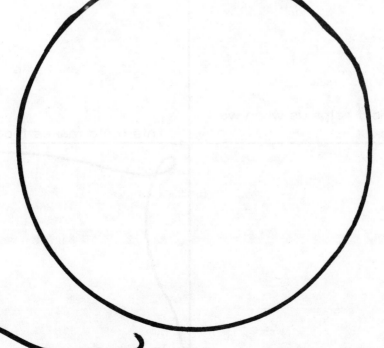

Choose another container of mold and compare it with
the bread mold. Write a paragraph or draw a picture
to show the comparison.

MOLDY OLDY

Draw a picture showing an example of each mold by using the reference material on the bulletin board.

This mold can be eaten.	This mold is an enemy.
This mold helps us when we are sick.	This mold makes food spoil.
This mold can grow on cotton material.	In this space make a list of places where you have seen mold growing

MOLDY OLDY

Keep a daily record to observe a mold colony. Use the microscope.

The <u>first day</u> put material in container, sprinkle it with water, and cover it.

The <u>second day</u> begin your daily record and continue to observe and record for five days.

Include in your record:

    A. A picture of your mold colony each day showing the change and a few sentences describing:

        1. The color of the mold
        2. The size of the mold
        3. The shape of the mold
        4. The odor of the mold

Jan. 23

This mold is green. It is as small as a pin. It is a circle. It smells stronger.

Try growing some different kinds of mold at home.

MOLDY OLDY

You are on a mold hunt. On how many different things can you find mold growing? Mold is never found on certain items. Let's see how well you do on the mold hunt!

Mold Grows On:

1. _____

2. _____

3. _____

4. _____

5. _____

6. _____

7. _____

8. _____

9. _____

10. _____

Mold Never Grows On:

1. _____

2. _____

3. _____

4. _____

5. _____

6. _____

7. _____

8. _____

9. _____

10. _____

Using the lists above, draw a conclusion about where you might find mold and where you won't find it.

_____

_____

_____

_____

_____

Use a resource book to see if the conclusion you have reached is correct.

MOLDY OLDY

Choose three containers of mold. In the boxes draw the material the mold is growing on. Answer the questions below:

```
┌──────────────┐   ┌──────────────┐   ┌──────────────┐
│              │   │              │   │              │
│              │   │              │   │              │
│              │   │              │   │              │
│              │   │              │   │              │
└──────────────┘   └──────────────┘   └──────────────┘
```

1. The color of the mold is:

_____   _____   _____

2. How many different shades of color are there?

_____   _____   _____

3. Which is the lightest?
   The darkest?

_____   _____   _____

4. Is the mold as large as a dime?
   A quarter? A pin?

_____   _____   _____

5. Is it shaped most like a circle?
   A square? An oval?

_____   _____   _____

6. Which smells the worst? The least?

_____   _____   _____

7. Which mold has grown the fastest? _____

8. Why has it grown faster? _____

Go back to the same mold several days later and see if the observations you made above have changed. If so, record the changes.

Mystery Maps

PURPOSE:

> After completing this center, the student should be able to make and read different kinds of maps.

MATERIALS:

Illustration and title
Activity sheets
Crayons, drawing paper
Large map of the United States
Current newspapers

PROCEDURE:

1. Place all materials in the center.

2. Verbally introduce the center to enable the student to complete the activities independently.

3. Provide time for evaluation of each completed activity and record individual student progress.

4. Make provisions for filing or displaying completed activities.

CALLING ALL CATS

College Avenue

Broadway Street

Washington Ave.

Church Street

Church St.

Rolling River

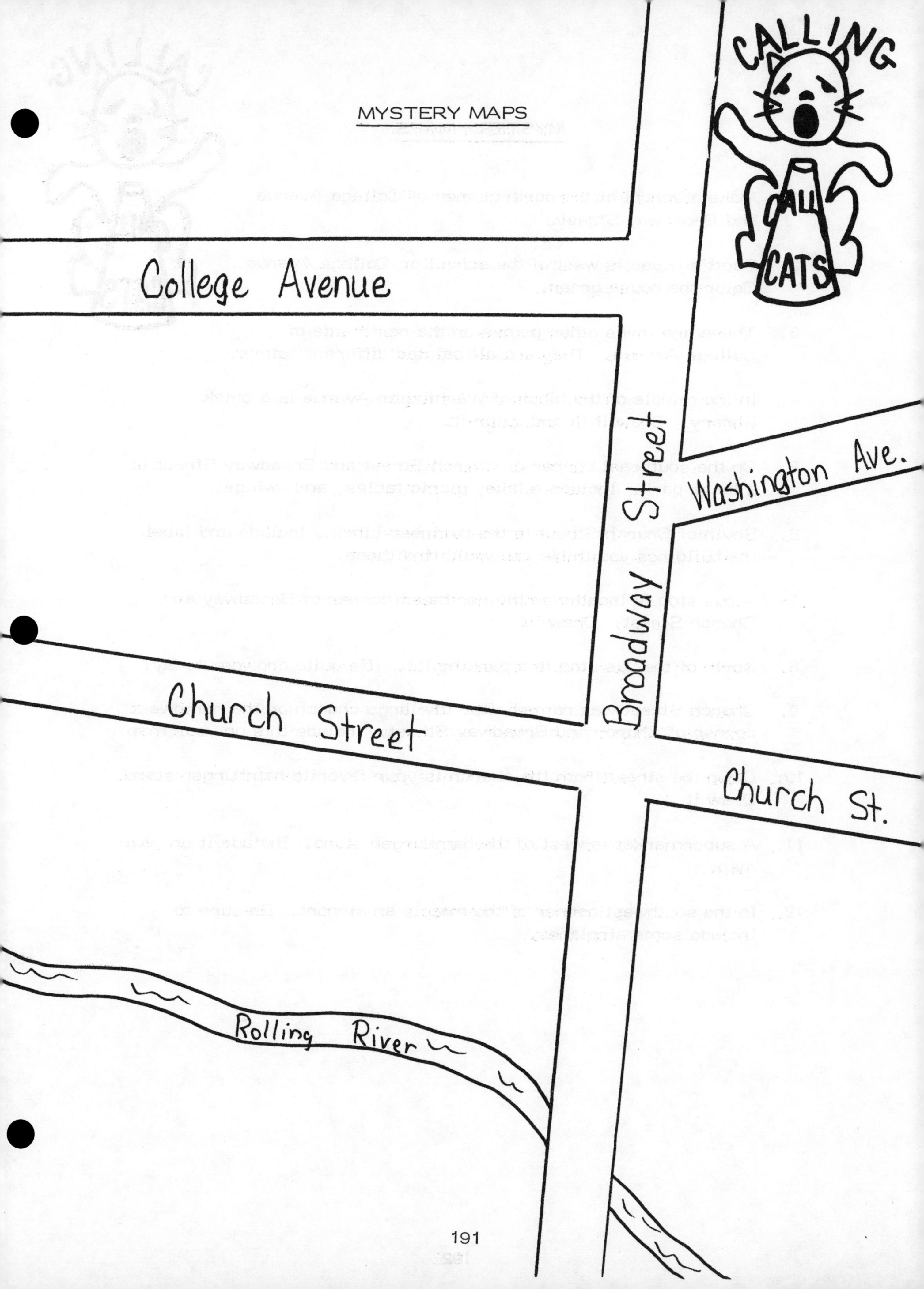

MYSTERY MAPS

1. Make a school at the north corner of College Avenue
    and Broadway Street.

2. Scott's house is west of the school on College Avenue.
    Color the house green.

3. There are three other homes on the north side of
    College Avenue. They are all painted different colors.

4. In the middle of the block of Washington Avenue is a brick
    library. Draw it in and color it.

5. On the southeast corner of Church Street and Broadway Street is
    a large park. Include a lake, picnic tables, and swings.

6. South of Church Street is the business block. Include and label
    the buildings you think you would find there.

7. A bus stop is located on the northeast corner of Broadway and
    Church Street. Draw it.

8. North of the bus stop is a parking lot. It's quite crowded today.

9. Church Street was named after the large church on the northwest
    corner of Church and Broadway Street. Include this on your map.

10. Down the street from the church is your favorite hamburger stand.
    Draw it.

11. A supermarket is west of the hamburger stand. Include it on your
    map.

12. In the southwest corner of the map is an airport. Be sure to
    include some airplanes.

MYSTERY MAPS

In the space below draw a map of the route you travel to get to school. Include the streets and their names, and the buildings and houses you pass.

On a large sheet of drawing paper draw a map of your bedroom at home. Redecorate by making it the colors you would like it to be.

MYSTERY MAPS

1. What kind of weather is your state having? _____
2. Would it be a good time to take a vacation in Florida? _____
   Why? _____
3. Name the states on the west coast. _____
   What kind of weather are they having? _____
4. What states are having two kinds of weather? _____
5. What weather is the state north of Kansas having? _____
6. Are more states having snow or rain? _____
7. What is the weather like in Ohio? _____
8. If you lived in Idaho, what would you need to wear outside? ____
   _____
9. What is the weather like in the states bordering Michigan? ____
10. If you were traveling from Montana to New Mexico, what kind of
    weather would you find? _____

Using the weather map in the newspaper, describe the weather
in the eastern states and the weather in the southern states.

MYSTERY MAPS

Using "Super Cat" map, complete these sentences.

1. Which state is north of Texas? _____

2. Which state is east of Montana? _____

3. Which states are north of Florida? _____

    _____

4. Which state is south of Iowa? _____

5. Which states are east of California? _____

6. Which states are north of Nevada? _____

7. Which state is between New Mexico and Wyoming? _____

8. Which state is south of Oklahoma? _____

9. Which state is between Illinois and Ohio? _____

10. Which states are west of Idaho? _____

11. Which state is north of North Carolina? _____

12. Which state is south of Nebraska? _____

13. Which states are west of Arizona? _____

14. Which states are east of New York? _____

15. Name all the states that border your state. _____

    _____

    _____

Choose a state you would like to visit. Write the names of
all the states you would go through to get there.

MYSTERY MAPS

North

West

South

East

1. Alabama	18. Louisiana	35. Ohio
2. Alaska	19. Maine	36. Oklahoma
3. Arizona	20. Maryland	37. Oregon
4. Arkansas	21. Massachusetts	38. Pennsylvania
5. California	22. Michigan	39. Rhode Island
6. Colorado	23. Minnesota	40. South Carolina
7. Connecticut	24. Mississippi	41. South Dakota
8. Delaware	25. Missouri	42. Tennessee
9. Florida	26. Montana	43. Texas
10. Georgia	27. Nebraska	44. Utah
11. Hawaii	28. Nevada	45. Vermont
12. Idaho	29. New Hampshire	46. Virginia
13. Illinois	30. New Jersey	47. Washington
14. Indiana	31. New Mexico	48. West Virginia
15. Iowa	32. New York	49. Wisconsin
16. Kansas	33. North Carolina	50. Wyoming
17. Kentucky	34. North Dakota	

No Laughing Matter

PURPOSE: After completing this center, the student
            should be able to identify the different
            properties of matter.

MATERIALS: Illustration and title
            Refer to the activity sheets for the materials
            needed for experiments and for optional
            activities.

PROCEDURE: 1. Place all materials in the center.

            2. Introduce the center to enable the student
                to complete activities independently.

            3. Provide time for evaluation of each completed
                activity and record individual student progress.

            4. Provide instructions to enable each student
                to make a laboratory booklet using the
                activity sheets and optional activities.

NO LAUGHING MATTER

Matter is anything that takes up space and has weight.
The three phases of matter are: solid, liquid and gas.

Look around the classroom and list the different kinds
of matter. Classify them according to solid, liquid, or gas.

Kinds of Matter	Solid	Liquid	Gas
pencil	×		

solid

liquid

gas

NO LAUGHING MATTER

Equipment: Plastic bag of water
               Plastic bag of air
               Wooden block

Directions: Examine the three types of matter and list
               the properties that you can discover about
               each one. Use your five senses to discover
               the properties. Some properties will be
               the same and others will be different.

Water	Air	Block

Prove that water, air, and the block occupy space and have
weight.

NO LAUGHING MATTER

Volume is the amount of space any matter occupies.
Volume is a property.

Equipment: brick
              balloon, coke bottle, prescription pill bottle,
               jelly jar
              pint, quart, 1/2 gallon container for water

Brick: Measure the brick.

	Length	Width	Height
In learning center			
In hallway			
Outside			

Did the solid change shape
as it was moved? _____

Balloon: Fill the balloon with
          air.
          Will the air in the
          balloon fit into each
          bottle? _____

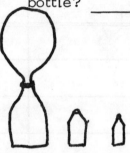

Did the air change shape to fit
each container? _____

Fill a pint container with water.
Put the water in the quart container.
Next put the water in a 1/2-gallon
container.

 pt.   qt.   ½ gal.

Did the water change
shapes as it was put in
different containers?

_____

Matter can change from one phase to another. Heat and cold
can affect this change. Make a list of matter that
temperature can change.

NO LAUGHING MATTER

What is matter made of? If you could take apart all matter you would find that it is made of elements. Elements are the building blocks of matter.

Some elements are gas:	Some are solids:	Some are liquids:
1. oxygen	1. gold	1. mercury
2. _____	2. _____	2. _____
3. _____	3. _____	3. _____

Can you fill in the above blanks?

Elements combined are called compounds. Using matter, discover some compounds.

Materials needed: Nail, sponge, dish, water

1. Place the nail on the sponge in the dish. Add enough water so that the sponge is wet.

2. After several days, what happens?

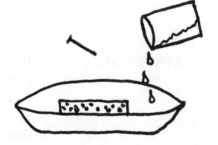

_____

_____

_____

Materials needed: hot plate, can with a little sugar, glass

1. Heat the sugar and hold a glass above it.

2. The sugar should begin changing, and the glass should have collected something. Write about it.

Look up the difference between a mixture and a compound. Make up an experiment that demonstrates this, and record your findings.

PURPOSE: | After completing this center, the student should be able to develop a better understanding of ocean resources.

MATERIALS:
Illustration and title
Pencils, drawing paper
Paint (tempera)
Finger paint, construction paper
Cardboard boxes (students bring their own)
Encyclopedias, resource books

PROCEDURE:

1. Prepare bulletin board to display sea animals for "Super Cat" option. Print directions for a diorama as given in "Smarty Cat" activity.

2. Place all materials in the center.

3. Introduce the center to enable the student to complete activities independently.

4. Provide time for evaluation of each completed activity and record individual student progress.

5. Make provision for filing or displaying completed activities.

OCEAN NOTION

Use a resource book to answer the questions below.

1. Oceanography is _____

   _____

2. List some equipment you will need to make a deep dive.

   _____

3. For what purpose are diving laboratories used? _____

   _____

4. List and describe three instruments for oceanography.

   _____   _____

   _____   _____

   _____   _____

5. List six minerals found in the ocean and on its floor.

   _____   _____

   _____   _____

6. Some microscopic plants in the ocean are:

   _____   _____

7. Sponges are _____.

8. Coral is _____.

9. Mollusks are a large group of sea animals. List some sea animals in this group.

   _____   _____   _____

10. The ocean is constantly changing because _____

    _____

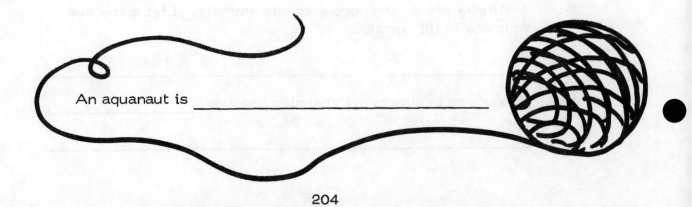

OCEAN NOTION

Match the words on the left with the definitions on the
right.   Put the letter beside the definition.

a.   oceanography   _____   oyster

b.   ports   _____   windows

c.   scuba   _____   tank of compressed air

d.   aqualung   _____   way of measuring water depth

e.   bathysphere   _____   organ for breathing

f.   snorkel   _____   study of the oceans

g.   fathoms   _____   brown algae

h.   algae   _____   danger to divers

i.   gills   _____   microscopic sea plants and animals

j.   mollusk   _____   tube that fits in a face mask

k.   mammal   _____   whale

l.   kelp   _____   skeleton of tiny sea animals

m.   plankton   _____   underwater breathing equipment

n.   invertebrate   _____   lowest form of plant life in sea

o.   coral   _____   animal without backbone

p.   bends   _____   underwater laboratory

An aquanaut is _____

OCEAN NOTION

Make a diorama of the sea. Take a cardboard box and cut
away one side and the top. Cover the three remaining sides
and the bottom of the box with blue construction paper.
Using different colored construction paper make plants
and animals of the sea.

Cut them out and paste them on the sides and bottom of
the box. Use your imagination and see how creative you
can be.

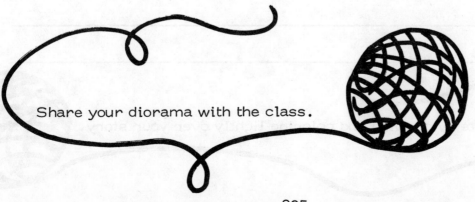

Share your diorama with the class.

OCEAN NOTION

Pretend you are an ocean diver. Write a story about an exciting dive you have made.

Why did you make the dive? Where did the dive take place? At what depth were you? Describe what you saw and did while you were underwater.

_____

_____

_____

_____

_____

_____

_____

_____

_____

_____

_____

_____

_____

Illustrate by drawing and coloring lightly over your story.

OCEAN NOTION

Choose a sea animal you are interested in. Look up information on the animal and make a report below.

Find out what the sea animal looks like, how large it is, what it eats, and some of its other habits.

My sea animal is _____.

_____

_____

_____

_____

_____

_____

_____

_____

_____

_____

_____

_____

Draw a picture of it here <u>exactly</u> as it looks.

Enlarge the picture of your sea animal on drawing paper.
Paint it and cut it out. Put it on the ocean bulletin board.

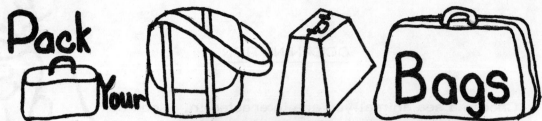

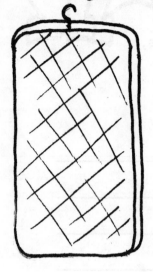

PURPOSE: After completing this center, the student
            should be able to use an encyclopedia as
            a resource tool to creatively plan a trip.

MATERIALS: Illustration and title
            Encyclopedias
            Drawing paper
            Tagboard, crayons

PROCEDURE: 1. Print directions for travel brochure
                found in "Super Cat" activity on a piece
                of tagboard.

            2. Place all materials in center.

            3. Introduce the center to enable the student
                to complete activities independently.

            4. Provide time for evaluation of each completed
                activity and record individual student progress.

            5. Make provision for filing or displaying
                completed activities.

PACK YOUR BAGS

Use an encyclopedia to complete this activity.

1.   Choose a country you would like to visit.

_____

2.   Why would you like to visit this country? _____

_____

3.   On what continent is it located? _____

4.   What countries border this country? _____

5.   What are the physical features of the land? _____

_____

_____

6.   What type of vegetation is found there? _____

_____

7.   What is the climate? _____

How does the country's location affect its climate? _____

_____

8.   Describe the people living there. _____

9.   How are the customs different from our own? _____

_____

10.   What is the type of government? _____

11.   What language is spoken? _____

12.   What type of transportation is used? _____

13.   What kind of animals are native to this country? _____

_____

14.   What types of food are eaten? _____

PACK YOUR BAGS

Now that you have chosen a country to visit, you will want a friend to travel with you.

Using the information you have learned about your country, convince your friend to make the trip with you. Write several paragraphs below describing the country so your friend will be interested.

_____

_____

_____

_____

_____

_____

_____

_____

_____

_____

_____

_____

_____

_____

_____

_____

Write a letter to the Bureau of Tourist Information to get additional information about this country.

PACK YOUR BAGS

Design a picture postcard and write a note to a friend telling about the country you plan to visit.

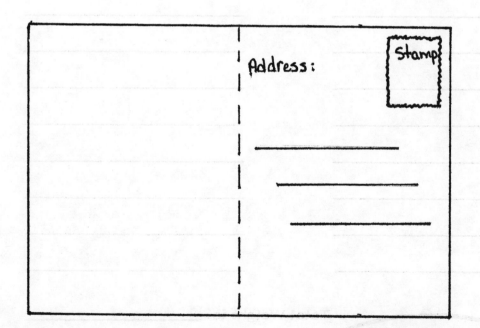

Address:

Stamp

Design a stamp for the postcard.

PACK YOUR BAGS

You will be leaving on your trip soon and you must begin planning what you will need to take with you. You will be allowed to take only forty pounds in your suitcase. The type of clothing you take will depend on the climate and your activities while there. List below the clothing and any other articles you will need. Estimate each article's weight.

Clothes & Articles	Estimated Weight
_____	_____
_____	_____
_____	_____
_____	_____
_____	_____
_____	_____
_____	_____
_____	_____
_____	_____
_____	_____
_____	_____
_____	_____

Total Weight is: _____

Draw pictures of all the articles you plan to take and estimate the number and size of the bags you will need to pack.

Using drawing paper and paints or crayons, make a travel brochure.

 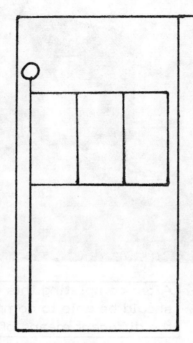 

Some things you may want to include:

Name and map of your country
Interesting places you visited
People and clothing
Recreational activities
Means of transportation
Animals
Foods and restaurants

Homes and hotels
Beautiful scenery
A government building
Flag
School
Famous landmark
Souvenirs

Design an attractive cover for your brochure, and fasten or staple it together.

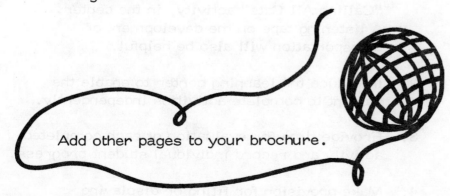

Add other pages to your brochure.

  Past Present Future

| PURPOSE: | After completing this center, the student should be able to compare and contrast the different means of transportation. |

MATERIALS: Illustration and title
                Activity sheets
                Encyclopedias or resource books
                Mural paper
                Paints
                Poster board
                Pockets for library cards
                Overhead projector
                Listening tape

PROCEDURE: 1.   Place all materials, including concentration
                  games prepared according to directions in
                  "Calling All Cats" activity, in the center.
                  A listening tape on the development of
                  transportation will also be helpful.

             2.   Introduce the learning center to enable the
                  student to complete activities independently.

             3.   Provide time for evaluation of each completed
                  activity and record individual student progress.

             4.   Make provision for filing or displaying
                  completed activities.

214

PAST – PRESENT – FUTURE

Using an encyclopedia or one of the resource books in the center, complete these sentences.

1. Man's earliest means of transportation was

    _____.

2. A travois was used by _____

    and it is _____.

3. When the Pilgrims first arrived in America, the best land

    routes were _____.

4. The Indians taught the early settlers to use two types of boats.

    These boats were _____ and _____.

5. List four means of transportation used by the early colonists.

    _____   _____

    _____   _____

6. Robert Fulton invented the _____

7. Why was his invention important? _____

    _____

8. Canals improved our transportation system by _____

    _____

    _____

9. The Tom Thumb was _____

10. List two advantages of railroad transportation. _____

    _____

    _____

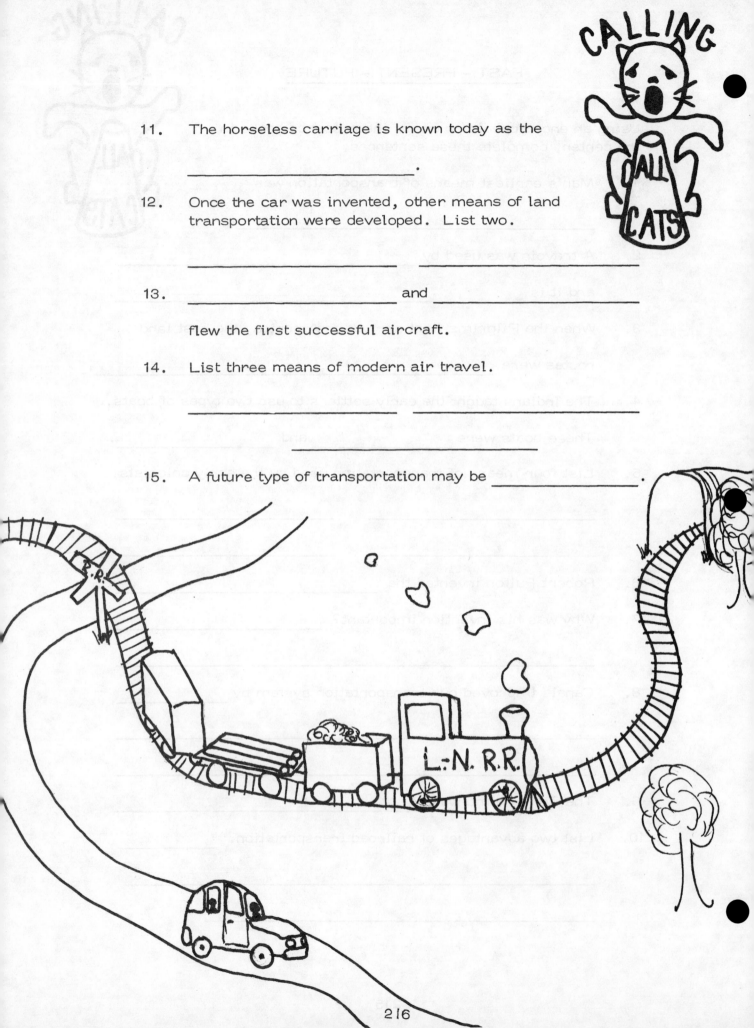

11. The horseless carriage is known today as the

    _____.

12. Once the car was invented, other means of land transportation were developed. List two.

    _____   _____

13. _____ and _____

    flew the first successful aircraft.

14. List three means of modern air travel.

    _____   _____

    _____

15. A future type of transportation may be _____.

PAST – PRESE ┌ – FUTURE

Concentration Game:

Use one colored piece of poster board and library 3" x 5" index cards to make the game board.

Directions for Concentration Game: This game is for two players. There are two matching cards. Draw two cards. If they match, the player keeps them. If the cards do not match, the player puts them back and tries to remember where they are. The players continue to draw cards until there are no more cards. The one with the most cards wins. The important thing is to concentrate on where the cards are placed.

PAST – PRESENT – FUTURE

Ideas to put on cards for Concentration Game:

Land	Walking
Water	Ocean liner
Air	Space ship
Land	Automobile
Water	Submarine
Air	Dirigible
Land	Bicycle
Water	Kayak
Air	Balloon
Water	Canoe
Land	Train

PAST – PRESENT – FUTURE

Pretend you are an inventor in the year 2050. Invent
a new means of transportation.   Draw it below:

Tell how it moves. _____

_____

_____

_____

Draw and label the materials
the invention is made of.

Draw and label the tools needed
to make this machine.

Using tempera, paint your invention on the mural.
Put it in the correct time zone.

PAST – PRESENT – FUTURE

List ten <u>present</u> means of transportation.

_____   _____

_____   _____

_____   _____

_____   _____

_____   _____

Pretend you have just won a trip to Hawaii. Plan the means of transportation you will use. Write about the transportation you will use to explore the island once you are there.

_____

_____

_____

_____

_____

_____

_____

_____

_____

_____

Select one means of present transportation to add to the transportation mural.

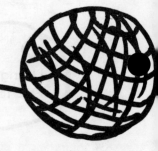

PAST – PRESENT – FUTURE

Think of at least twenty different means of transportation. Choose a type of transportation you are interested in. Use the encyclopedia or a resource book and write a short report on it.

_____

_____

_____

_____

_____

_____

_____

_____

_____

_____

_____

_____

_____

_____

_____

_____

Paint your means of transportation on the mural. Put it in the correct time period.

Peabody Pirates

PURPOSE:	After completing this center, the student should be better able to follow directions.

MATERIALS: Illustration and title
Tagboard
Pencils
Activity sheets
Crayons

PROCEDURE:

1. Prepare Treasure Hunt according to directions given in "Calling All Cats" activity.

2. Place all materials in the center.

3. Introduce the center to enable the student to complete activities independently.

4. Provide time for evaluation of each completed activity and record individual student progress.

5. Make provisions for filing or displaying completed activities.

PEABODY PIRATES

Treasure Hunt:

1. Prepare a set of Treasure Hunt clues.
   The students must find and follow the
   clues that will eventually lead them to a
   treasure chest filled with candy and other
   tokens.

2. The clues may be printed on strips of tagboard and
   hidden in the room.

Some examples might be:

Go to the reading
shelf and find the
clue in the third
red book.

Look under John's desk
for your next clue.

On p. 63 in a "B"
encyclopedia find
your next clue.

3. New directions will be needed every day.

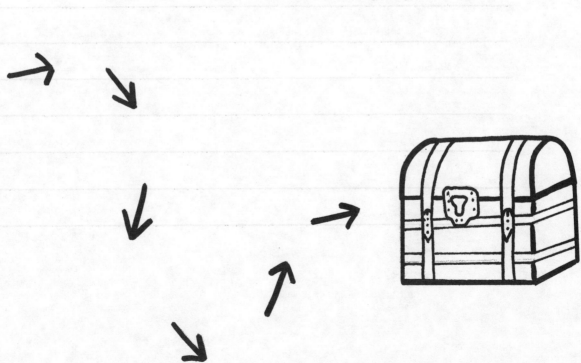

PEABODY PIRATES

Today you have just become a pirate. What is your name? Where do you live? Do you own a ship? What adventure are you planning? Where will you go and will you be alone?

Write a story telling about yourself and the exciting adventures you are having.

_____

_____

_____

_____

_____

_____

_____

_____

_____

_____

_____

_____

PEABODY PIRATES

Follow the maze to reach the treasure chest.

Draw a picture of yourself as a pirate.

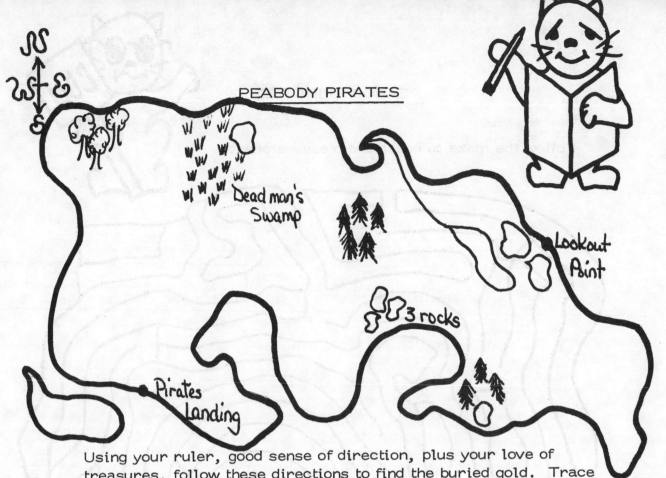

PEABODY PIRATES

Using your ruler, good sense of direction, plus your love of treasures, follow these directions to find the buried gold. Trace your route.

1. Starting at the most southern tip of the island, make an X and sail North exactly 1 inch.

2. Go directly west 1-1/2 inches and spend the night there. Mark the spot.

3. Moving 2-1/2 inches directly west, you meet more pirates and nearly get your map stolen.

4. Sail 1 inch north and keep travelling 2 inches north. You are now at _____.

5. Sail north 1 inch and sail west 2 inches, then south 1/2 inch. Travel south another inch and spend the night. Mark it. You are getting closer to the treasure.

6. Travel exactly 2-1/2 inches south, then 1 inch east. You are at _____. Beware!

7. Travel 1-1/2 inches north, then 2-1/2 inches east. Rest.

8. Go 1-3/4 inches east and you've arrived. Start digging and circle the place where the treasure is.

You've opened the chest and there isn't buried treasure. What is there? Write a paragraph telling what you've found.

PEABODY PIRATES

Following all the directions below, make a map of the island.

1. Put a direction indicator in the top righthand corner.

2. A forest of fruit trees is in the northwest corner of the island.

3. Pine trees grow on the eastern end of the island.

4. Mountains are found in the middle of the island.

5. Flowing east from the mountains is a river; it forms a lake near the northeast coast.

6. The southwest corner of the island contains a swamp; there are many low grasses around it.

7. Make a good place to harbor your ship. Label it.

8. As a pirate, where would you live? Mark it on the map.

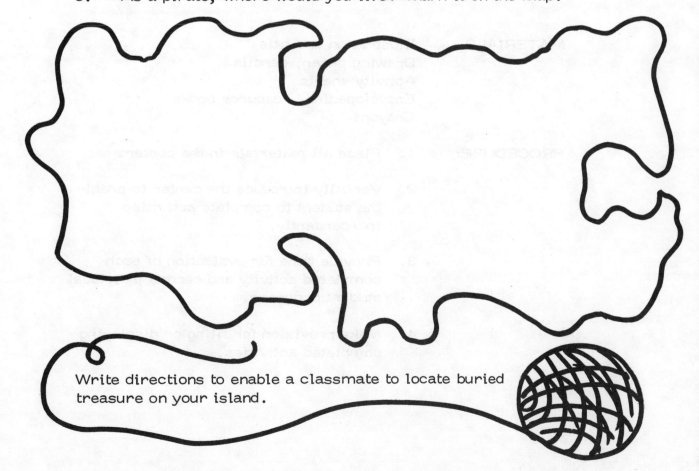

Write directions to enable a classmate to locate buried treasure on your island.

Pollution Solution

PURPOSE: After completing this center, the student
            should be aware of some steps being
            taken to solve pollution problems.

MATERIALS: Illustration and title
            Drawing paper, pencils
            Activity sheets
            Encyclopedias, resource books
            Crayons

PROCEDURE: 1. Place all materials in the center.

            2. Verbally introduce the center to enable
                the student to complete activities
                independently.

            3. Provide time for evaluation of each
                completed activity and record individual
                student progress.

            4. Make provision for filing or displaying
                completed activities.

POLLUTION SOLUTION

Use an encyclopedia or one of the resource books in
the center to help you complete the following sentences.

1. Environmental pollution is _____

    _____

2. Four kinds of pollution are _____,

    _____, _____,

    and _____.

3. Air pollution can cause _____.

4. Water pollution can cause _____.

5. The development of technology has caused pollution by

    _____

6. Our economy has caused pollution by _____

    _____

7. Convenience or social pollution is caused by _____

    _____

8. Four ways man is trying to control pollution are

    _____, _____

    _____, and _____

9. Environmental Protection Agency is _____

    _____

10. Earth Day was _____

11. Earth Day was important because _____

    _____

POLLUTION SOLUTION

Use an encyclopedia to find answers to the questions below. You may also need to use a resource book to help you answer some of the questions.

*1.   What is environment? _____

_____

2.   Now describe your environment. _____

_____

_____

3.   Name some other environments. _____

_____

Man must be able to adapt to the environment in order to live.

4.   How has man had to adapt to live in space? _____

_____

_____

5.   How does he live in the North or South Pole? _____

_____

Often when man decides to live or play somewhere changes take place in the environment.

6.   What happens to plants and animals in a forest when man builds houses there? _____

_____

7.   An amusement park built near a lake can change the environment. How? _____

_____

Have you had to adapt your living for a while or permanently?
Write a paragraph or draw a picture explaining this.

POLLUTION SOLUTION

1. Recycling is _____

    _____

2. Three kinds of wastes that can be recycled are

    _____, _____

    and _____

3. Choose one kind of waste that can be recycled, and describe

    the process. You may use a resource book for reference.

    _____

    _____

    _____

    _____

    _____

    _____

    _____

    _____

4. Tell how the material can be used after the recycling process.

    _____

    _____

    _____

    _____

Draw a picture showing the recycling process of the material
you selected.

POLLUTION SOLUTION

Pretend you have just been elected mayor of a large city. One of the first jobs you will be asked to do is to try to solve the city's pollution problem. Write a newspaper story telling what the causes of pollution are and giving your suggestions for eliminating the problems.

_____

_____

_____

_____

_____

_____

_____

_____

_____

_____

_____

_____

_____

Using an encyclopedia or resource book, list some ways the government or private organizations have helped solve pollution problems.

POLLUTION SOLUTION

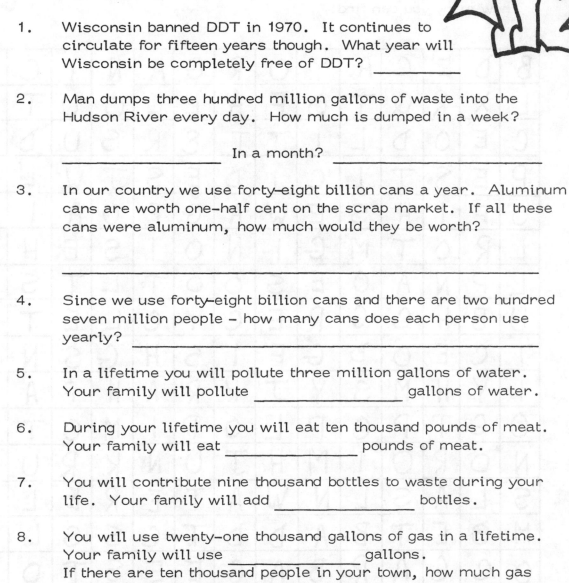

Pollution affects all of us, and unfortunately we do some polluting ourselves. Take a look at these facts and do some figuring for yourself.

1. Wisconsin banned DDT in 1970. It continues to circulate for fifteen years though. What year will Wisconsin be completely free of DDT? _____

2. Man dumps three hundred million gallons of waste into the Hudson River every day. How much is dumped in a week?

    _____ In a month? _____

3. In our country we use forty-eight billion cans a year. Aluminum cans are worth one-half cent on the scrap market. If all these cans were aluminum, how much would they be worth?

    _____

4. Since we use forty-eight billion cans and there are two hundred seven million people – how many cans does each person use yearly? _____

5. In a lifetime you will pollute three million gallons of water. Your family will pollute _____ gallons of water.

6. During your lifetime you will eat ten thousand pounds of meat. Your family will eat _____ pounds of meat.

7. You will contribute nine thousand bottles to waste during your life. Your family will add _____ bottles.

8. You will use twenty-one thousand gallons of gas in a lifetime. Your family will use _____ gallons.
    If there are ten thousand people in your town, how much gas will they use in a lifetime? _____

Count the number of cars and number of passengers that travel by your house in a 30-minute period. If each car carried three passengers, how many fewer cars would be necessary?

POLLUTION SOLUTION

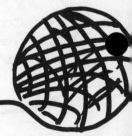

Circle all the words below that relate to pollution and ecology. The words can be horizontal, vertical, on the diagonal or reversed. There are thirty-three words. See how many you can find.

B	D	E	C	A	Y	O	R	G	A	N	I	C	A
L	X	R	Q	T	O	F	A	L	L	O	U	T	R
C	E	O	D	L	I	T	T	E	R	S	U	D	S
P	E	S	T	I	C	I	D	E	S	J	W	L	R
O	F	I	H	S	E	W	A	G	E	O	A	I	R
L	R	O	T	M	G	I	N	O	I	S	E	H	S
L	P	N	A	O	E	S	O	O	T	L	T	S	I
U	B	H	C	G	R	E	C	Y	C	L	E	T	N
T	C	E	O	D	G	F	I	S	H	G	S	N	V
I	Y	H	M	S	Y	J	K	R	A	H	F	A	E
O	G	T	P	O	P	L	O	P	I	M	O	T	R
N	O	R	O	I	M	H	J	U	N	K	R	U	S
S	L	A	S	L	N	W	A	T	E	R	E	L	I
M	O	E	T	B	A	D	D	T	C	S	S	L	O
O	C	G	A	R	B	A	G	E	E	S	T	O	N
K	E	N	V	I	R	O	N	M	E	N	T	P	R
E	P	R	E	M	E	R	C	U	R	Y	S	T	U

Use a large sheet of drawing paper to make a poster promoting anti-pollution. You may want to use paper and paste, crayons or colored chalk from the art center.

234

Roatsy Oatsies

PURPOSE: After completing this center the student should be aware of the influence of mass media on the public.

MATERIALS: Illustration and title
                 Tagboard   Cardboard box
                 Paint   Crayons
                 Scissors   Pencils
                 Magic markers   Activity sheets
                 Roll of shelf paper   Magazines

PROCEDURE: 1. Place illustration, title, activity sheets, magazines, directions, art materials and shelf paper in the center.

                 2. Introduce the entire center so that the student will be able to complete activities independently according to directions.

                 3. Provide time for evaluation of each activity with the individual student.

                 4. Arrange small group discussion sessions and display areas for activities to be shared, and give instructions for filing other completed activities.

ROATSY OATSIES

Prepare a cardboard box to be used as a television set. Section a roll of shelf paper to provide a space for each student. When the roll is completed mount the roll on dowel rods and place in the box so it can be moved in sequence. You may want to tape the commercials.

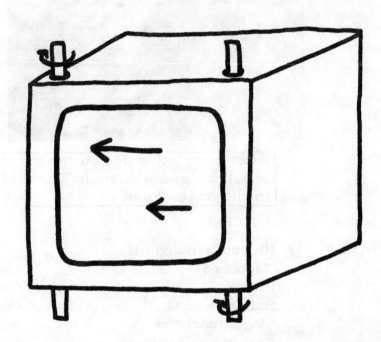

1. Create a product that you would like to advertise.

2. Sketch your advertisement on a piece of drawing paper as you would like it to appear on television.

3. Once you feel satisfied with your sketch, transfer it to the television roll. Remember this is color television.

4. Write a song or poem to accompany your picture.

5. When your picture appears on the television program screen, read or sing the commercial to accompany your picture.

ROATSY OATSIES

Cut one advertisement from the magazines. Study the advertisement to find answers for the questions below.

1.   What product is advertised? _____

2.   For what is the product used? _____

_____

3.   According to this advertisement, in what way could this pro-
      duct benefit you? _____

_____

4.   What is the first thing you noticed when you saw this adver-
      tisement? _____

5.   Why did you notice this first? _____

6.   Write the most important words in this advertisement. _____

_____

7.   How have the words in the advertisement been written to give
      them importance? _____

_____

8.   Is the price of the product given? _____

9.   Why do you think the price is or isn't given? _____

_____

10.   List at least three guidelines you think were used in writing
      the advertisement. (1) _____

      (2) _____   (3) _____

11.   How does the picture improve the advertisement? _____

_____

Using the same advertisement, paste only the picture from
the advertisement on drawing paper and write your own
advertisement.

ROATSY OATSIES

Study the lines from the advertisements and then
fill in the blanks to tell what is being advertised.
Draw and label the container the product comes in.

Cherry Chewies are great for
a snack and extra energy.

Super Go keeps your car
running great.

Beautiful Bubbles lets you take
the bath you'll never forget.

Soft and Dreamy catches those
sneezes and never hurts your nose.

Make up two of your own!

ROATSY OATSIES

Using the magazines, find two advertisements of one
product that is manufactured by two different companies.
Example: Toothpaste – Crest toothpaste
Ultra–Brite toothpaste

1.   What products are advertised? _____

2.   How are they used? _____

3.   According to these advertisements, would one of these pro-
      ducts benefit you more than the other? _____ How?

      _____

      _____

4.   Which of these advertisements would you notice first?

      _____

5.   Why did you notice it first? _____

6.   Which picture is more appealing in the advertisement? _____

      Why? _____

7.   Is there a difference in the style of printing? _____

      Which do you think is more appealing to the reader? _____

      _____

8.   Using the advertisements as a guide, which brand would you
      buy? _____

      Why? _____

      _____

Tonight, listen to radio and television commercials
and compare their styles of advertising. Write a
short paragraph comparing the two ways of advertising.

ROATSY OATSIES

A very fancy restaurant has just hired you to rewrite their menus so they will be more exotic. Make this food sound more enticing!

Luncheon Menu

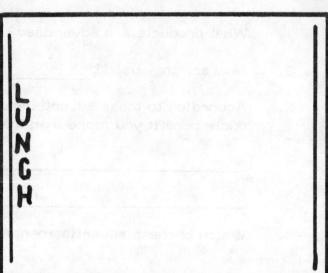

ham sandwich
beef sandwich
tomato soup
vegetable soup
stew
chicken salad
shrimp salad
iced tea
coffee
apple pie
ice cream

Dinner Menu

shrimp cocktail
tomato juice

steak
creamed chicken
pork chops

green beans
corn
french fries
tossed salad

cheese cake
hot fudge sundae

coffee

Prepare a menu for a restaurant you would like to own. Use a sheet of drawing paper and design the outside and inside.

ROATSY OATSIES

toothpaste	shampoo	cereal
soap	cologne	deodorant
soft drinks	gum	candy

Choose one of these products to advertise. Include
in your advertisement pictures, word gimmicks, and
any other information that will sell your product.

Compare your advertisement with another student who
selected the same product. Decide which advertisement
would make more people buy the product.

Sense -A- Rama

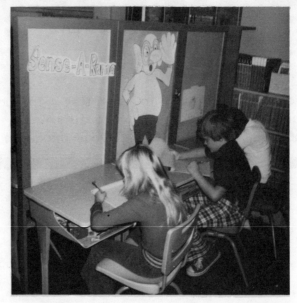

PURPOSE: | After completing this center, the student should be aware of the five senses and the importance of each one.

MATERIALS: Illustration and title
Popcorn
Activity sheets
Box with objects to feel
Bottles filled for students to smell

PROCEDURE: 1.   Prepare popcorn to use with "Cool Cat" activity. Place different objects in a covered box to be used with "Smarty Cat" activity. Prepare six covered bottles with different odors to be used with "Super Cat" activity.

2.   Place all materials in the center.

3.   Introduce the center to enable the student to complete activities independently.

4.   Provide time for evaluation of each completed activity and record individual student progress.

5.   Make provision for filing or displaying completed activities.

SENSE-A-RAMA

Sit quietly on the outside steps and listen for different sounds. Make a list of at least fifteen sounds you hear.

1. _____   9. _____

2. _____   10. _____

3. _____   11. _____

4. _____   12. _____

5. _____   13. _____

6. _____   14. _____

7. _____   15. _____

8. _____

Classify the sounds that you hear:

Happy Sounds	Sad Sounds	Working Sounds
_____	_____	_____
_____	_____	_____
_____	_____	_____
_____	_____	_____
_____	_____	_____

Unnecessary Sounds

_____	_____	_____
_____	_____	_____
_____	_____	

On the back of this paper tell how unnecessary sounds could be stopped.

SENSE-A-RAMA

Lucky you! Use the popcorn to answer these questions.

1. What does your sense of hearing tell you when making popcorn? _____

    _____

2. How did you know there was popcorn when you came into the room? _____

    _____

    What sense did you use? _____

3. Did the corn feel the same before it was popped as it did after it was popped? _____

    What sense did you use? _____

4. What does your sense of taste tell you about the popcorn?

    _____

5. Compare the corn before it was popped and after it was popped. Color: _____

    Size: _____

    Smell: _____

    Texture: _____

6. Use your sense of sight and describe what popcorn looks like to you. _____

    _____

    _____

On the back of the paper list the five senses. Beside each tell how important that sense is to you during a school day.

SENSE-A-RAMA

Put your hand in the box. Using your sense of touch,
see how many objects you can identify by feeling them.

Objects	Description

How do you use your sense of touch every day? On the
back of this paper, make a list of ways you use the sense
of touch.

SENSE-A-RAMA

Open each bottle and smell what is inside. Match the
number on the bottle to the number below. Tell what
you think causes each odor.

1. _____   2. _____

3. _____   4. _____

5. _____   6. _____

Which of the smells did you like? _____

_____

Which of the smells didn't you like? _____

Why? _____

List four things that would smell the same as No. 1.

1. _____   2. _____

3. _____   4. _____

List three things that smell the same as No. 6.

1. _____   2. _____   3. _____

What smells would you miss if you lost your sense of smell?

_____

Why is it good to have a sense of smell? _____

_____

Have you ever wished you didn't have your sense of smell? _____

Why? _____

On the back, write a paragraph that tells which sense you
think is the most important, and why.

246

Shady Shadows

PURPOSE: After completing this center, the student should understand what causes shadows, and be able to recognize objects from the shadows they cast.

MATERIALS: Illustration and title
Filmstrip or overhead projector
Writing paper, pencil
Construction paper
Flashlight
Four 3-dimensional geometric shapes
Box containing small objects
Cardtable or chair, piece of muslin
Several resource books on shadows

PROCEDURE: 1.   Make a shadow box following directions in "Cool Cat" activity. Prepare bulletin board for "Smarty Cat" activity. Stretch muslin or sheet over three legs of a cardtable or a chair for option on "Smarty Cat" activity.

2.   Place all materials in center.

3.   Introduce the center to enable the student to complete activities independently.

4.   Provide time for evaluation of each completed activity and record individual student progress.

5.   Make provision for filing or displaying activities.

SHADY SHADOWS

Choose a resource book from the center to help you to complete this activity sheet.

The title of the book is _____

_____ .

The author is _____ .

The length of the book is _____ .

Five interesting facts I learned about shadows are:

1. _____

    _____

2. _____

    _____

3. _____

    _____

4. _____

    _____

5. _____

    _____

I liked this book because _____

_____

_____

_____

SHADY SHADOWS

If light cannot go through an object, that object can cast
a shadow.

Draw four objects that can cast a shadow.
Draw two objects that cannot cast a shadow.

Bring one object from home that can cast a shadow and one
object that cannot cast a shadow. Share them with students
in the center.

SHADY SHADOWS

An overhead projector or a filmstrip projector can be used to project shadows. A simple shadow box can be made from a corrugated cardboard box. Remove two parallel sides of the box. Stretch muslin or white paper over one open side. Use a flashlight or filmstrip projector to cast the shadow from the other open side.

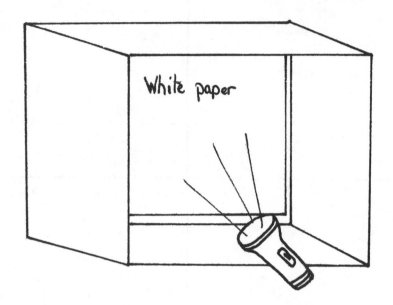

White paper

Provide a box with simple objects. These might include toys, household gadgets, school supplies or any objects you wish. Objects may be selected from the box and used in the shadow box to project shadows. Other students in the center may participate by guessing the object casting the shadow.

Bring different objects from home to cast shadows for your classmates to guess.

SHADY SHADOWS

Make a tree trunk with bare branches and put it on the bulletin board.

1. Turn on the overhead projector or filmstrip projector to focus the light on a plain wall or screen.

2. Experiment using your hands and arms to make shadow shapes.

3. Choose a shape that is interesting and ask a classmate to trace the shadow on construction paper.

4. Cut the shadow shape out and hang it on a branch of the shadow tree.

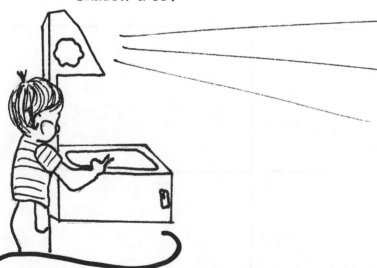

Every day a shadow play may be presented. Use your hands and arms to form shadow characters for a shadow play. You may wish to ask two or three other people to help you.

SHADY SHADOWS

Take the four geometric shapes and study them from
all sides. Draw the shadows you think they will cast.
When you have completed your drawings, put the
shapes in the shadow box or in front of the projector
to see what shape the shadow really is. Draw that
and compare!

Shadows you think the
Shapes have:

Actual Shadows:

Tell why you think your shadows are different from the
actual ones.

SHADY SHADOWS

Shadows are formed when light cannot go through an object. If the light source moves, the shape of the shadow will change. Show how the tree's shadow will change during the day by drawing it with a black crayon. You may need to look outside for some help.

8 a.m.

Noon

4 p.m.

Find out what a sundial is and how it works. Write a paragraph explaining this.

Spring Styles

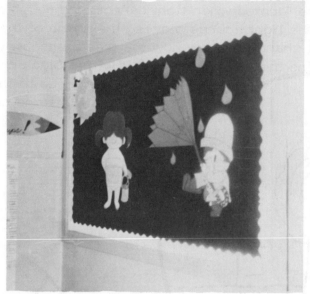

PURPOSE: After completing this center, the student
            should be able to identify and tell the origin
            of different fabrics.

MATERIALS: Illustration and title
            Printed directions
            Activity sheets
            Encyclopedias, resource books
            Samples of different kinds of fabric
            Clothing catalogue

PROCEDURE: 1. Place samples of different kinds of material
                in a box to use with "Cool Cat" activity.

            2. Place all materials in center.

            3. Introduce the center to enable the student
                to complete activities independently.

            4. Provide time for evaluation of each completed
                activity and record individual student progress.

            5. Make provision for filing or displaying completed
                activities.

SPRING STYLES

We wear clothes made from many different materials.
Some come from plants. Some come from animals, and
some are man-made. Use one of the resource books or an
encyclopedia to list six different types of material used for
clothing. Summarize in two or three sentences what you
learned about each kind of material.

1. _____

_____

_____

2. _____

_____

_____

3. _____

_____

_____

4. _____

_____

_____

5. _____

_____

_____

6. _____

_____

_____

SPRING STYLES

Using the information you listed in the "Calling All Cats" activity:

1. List the six kinds of material.
2. Draw a picture showing the origin of this material.
3. From the material box, find a sample of each kind of material listed. Paste it beside the picture.

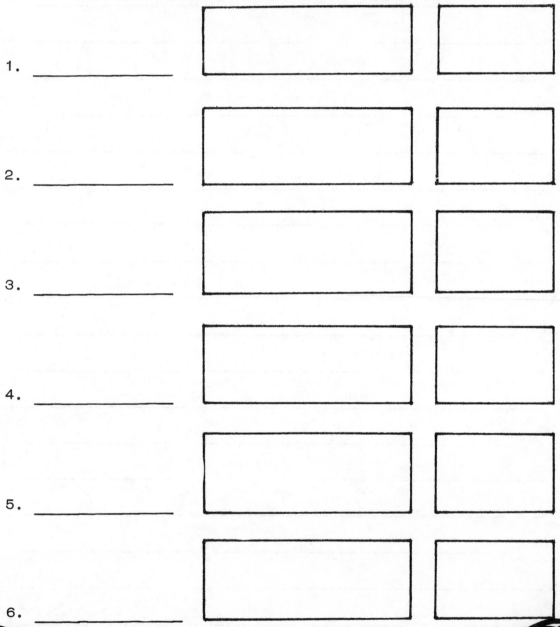

1. _____

2. _____

3. _____

4. _____

5. _____

6. _____

Design an outfit for yourself. Draw one outfit you might wear for sports or play, or one you might wear for dress. Be sure to color your outfit.

SPRING STYLES

Choose two kinds of material and draw a story picture
showing the process necessary before it is ready to be worn.

Design a piece of fabric for each kind of material you drew
a story picture for. Draw a picture of the object of clothing
you would like to have made from this fabric.

SPRING STYLES

The weather is turning warm and you need some new clothes. You have $100 to spend. Look in the catalogue and make a list of the clothes you want to buy. Then tell what kind of material the clothing is made from.

How much does it cost?

Clothing	Type of Material Used	Cost
_____	_____	_____
_____	_____	_____
_____	_____	_____
_____	_____	_____
_____	_____	_____
_____	_____	_____
_____	_____	_____
_____	_____	_____
_____	_____	_____
_____	_____	_____
_____	_____	_____
_____	_____	_____
_____	_____	_____

Add the cost of all the clothes you have bought to see if you have any money left over.

I spent _____.

SPRING STYLES

Do you wonder how people in other countries dress? Look in the encyclopedia and find the different kinds of clothing worn by people in other countries.

1. Choose one country that interests you.
2. Tell about the kind of clothing worn there.
3. From what material is it made?
4. Why is this kind of material used?

Write a paragraph summarizing what you learned.

_____

_____

_____

_____

_____

_____

_____

_____

_____

_____

_____

_____

_____

_____

Draw a picture of a person dressed in this clothing.

The BIG Bite

PURPOSE:

> After completing this center, the student
> should be aware of the importance of good
> health habits.

MATERIALS:
Illustration and title
Resource books, encyclopedias
Activity sheets
Calorie chart, four food groups chart
Drawing paper

PROCEDURE:

1. Place all materials in the center.

2. Introduce the center to enable the student to complete the activities independently.

3. Provide time for evaluation of each completed activity and record individual student progress.

4. Make provision for filing or displaying completed activities.

THE BIG BITE

Minerals and vitamins are necessary for good health and strong bodies. Use one of the resource books to find how each vitamin or mineral helps the body. Then identify the food source of each mineral or vitamin.

1. Calcium helps build _____.

   Source – _____

2. Iron helps build _____.

   Source – _____

3. Protein helps build _____.

   Source – _____

4. Carbohydrates help build _____.

   Source – _____

5. Vitamin A helps build _____.

   Source – _____

6. Vitamin B helps build _____.

   Source – _____

7. Vitamin C helps build _____.

   Source – _____

8. Vitamin D helps build _____.

   Source – _____

9. Water helps _____.

   Source – _____

10. If you left one of these minerals or vitamins out of your diet, how would it affect you?

    _____

THE BIG BITE

Using a resource book, find out how important rest is to the body and what happens when you do not get enough rest.

Write a paragraph including some good ways to rest.

_____

_____

_____

_____

_____

_____

_____

_____

_____

_____

_____

_____

_____

_____

_____

Make a list of the symptoms you might have if you fail to get enough rest.

262

THE BIG BITE

Using a resource book, find out how important exercise is to the body, and what happens when you do not get enough exercise. Write a paragraph or a poem about the importance of exercise.

_____

_____

_____

_____

_____

_____

_____

_____

_____

_____

_____

_____

_____

_____

Draw a picture of your favorite way to exercise.

THE BIG BITE

You are the proud owner of a snack shop.

1. What are you going to name it?

   _____

2. Make the sign for your shop below.

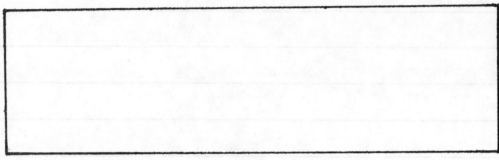

3. Where is your shop located? _____

4. How many tables do you have in it? _____

5. How many people can you serve at one time? _____

   Why? _____

6. What kinds of snacks will you serve? _____

   _____

7. Make a menu with the prices you will charge.

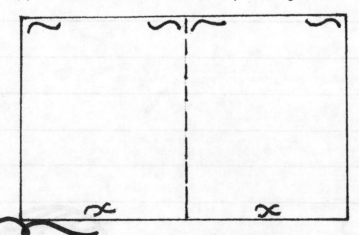

8. List all the people you will need to help in the operation of your shop.

   _____

   _____

   _____

If your snack shop served dieters only, how would you change your menu? Write a new menu.

THE BIG BITE

1. Use the encyclopedia to find out what a calorie is.

_____

2. Plan a full day's menu including snacks! Use the
   daily requirements from the four basic food groups to help
   you. List the number of calories in each food. (Use the
   calorie counter.)

   Breakfast: Calories:

   _____   _____

   _____   _____

   _____   _____

   Lunch:

   _____   _____

   _____   _____

   _____   _____

   Dinner:

   _____   _____

   _____   _____

   _____   _____

   Snacks:

   _____   _____

   _____   _____

                                          Total _____

How many calories does your body require daily? _____

Look up some of your favorite foods and see how many
calories they have. List them.

265

This is Your Life

PURPOSE: After completing this center, the student should be able to envision an improved self-concept.

MATERIALS: Illustration and title
Activity sheets
Pencils
Drawing paper
Crayons

PROCEDURE:
1. Place all materials in the center.

2. Verbally introduce the center to enable the student to complete activities independently.

3. Provide time for evaluation of each completed activity and record individual student progress.

4. Make provision for filing or displaying completed activities.

THIS IS YOUR LIFE

Fill in the vital information on this Identification Card:

Name _____
Address _____
City and State _____
Telephone No. _____ Zip Code _____
Male or Female _____ Age _____
Height _____ Weight _____
Color of Hair _____ Color of Eyes _____
School _____ Grade _____
Parents' Name _____
If I am not at home, you will find me at _____

Years ago, people had shields designed for them to indicate their tastes and activities. Using the directions below, color in your shield.

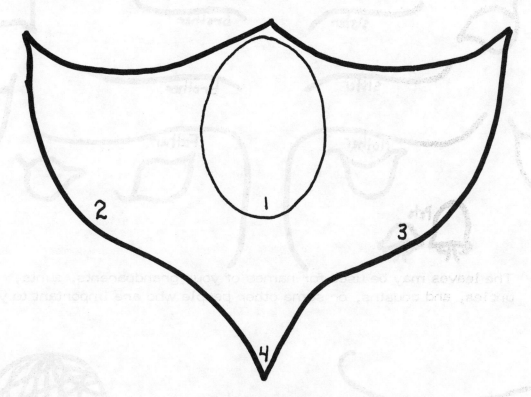

1.   Picture of you
2.   Favorite toy or book
3.   Favorite activity
4.   A design using your favorite colors

THIS IS YOUR LIFE

My first name is _____.

My last name is _____.

My middle name is _____.

My nickname is _____.

If I could change my name it would be _____.

This is my family:

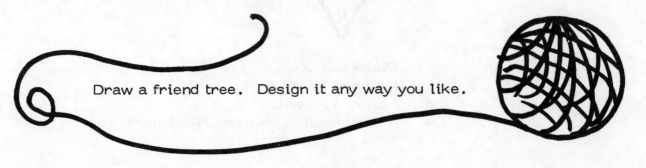

sister   brother

sister   brother

sister   brother

Mother   Father

Pets

The leaves may be used for names of your grandparents, aunts, uncles, and cousins, or some other people who are important to you.

Draw a friend tree. Design it any way you like.

THIS IS YOUR LIFE

People are always wishing to change things. This is your chance!

If you could change your

Appearance, it would be: _____

_____

Family, it would be: _____

_____

School, it would be: _____

_____

Teacher, it would be: _____

_____

Friends, they would be: _____

_____

House, it would be: _____

_____

Food, it would be: _____

_____

Clothes, they would be: _____

_____

Free Time, it would be: _____

_____

A rule or law, it would be: _____

_____

Draw a picture to illustrate one of these changes.

THIS IS YOUR LIFE

An autobiography is your life story written by you.
Write your autobiography. You will want to include
your family, the different places you have lived,
interesting things you have done, hobbies, your likes
and dislikes, and anything else important to your
life story.

_____

_____

_____

_____

_____

_____

_____

_____

_____

_____

_____

_____

_____

_____

_____

_____

Draw a family portrait.

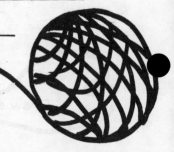

Wanted: Dead or Alive

PURPOSE: After completing this center, the student should be able to identify and classify living and non-living things.

MATERIALS: Illustration and title
             Activity sheets
             Tagboard squares
             Printed study guide
             Box

PROCEDURE: 1.   Place all materials in center. Print the words listed in "Cool Cat" activity on 1" x 2" tagboard cards. Put the cards in a box. Make a study guide explaining living and non-living things.

             2.   Introduce the center by taking students outside to observe and discuss living and non-living things.

             3.   Provide time for evaluation of each completed activity and record individual student progress.

             4.   Make provision for filing or displaying completed activities.

WANTED: DEAD OR ALIVE

Take a walking field trip around the school grounds
or in the neighborhood. Make a list of all living and
non-living things you see. Classify them as living or
non-living by checking the appropriate column.

List of things seen	Living	Non-living

When you return from the field trip, have a class discussion about
the observation of living and non-living things.

WANTED: DEAD OR ALIVE

Directions:

Sort the cards into stacks of living and non-living things.

starfish	truck	doll

shoe	leaf	bubble gum	flag

shrimp	purse	cow	train

submarine	car	plastic flower	whale

squid	building	human being	mushroom

tomato plant	eagle	jeep	rock

spoon	onion	desk	bumblebee

Add one card for living things and one card for non-living things to the game.

273

WANTED: DEAD OR ALIVE

1. Tell how the two items above are different.

_____

_____

2. How are the above two items alike?

_____

_____

3. How are the shoe and house alike?

_____

_____

4. How are the pencil and the boy different?

_____

_____

5. From the conclusions you have made above, tell what all living things have in common. There should be four.

(a) _____

(b) _____

(c) _____

(d) _____

Cut out a magazine picture and glue it on a sheet of drawing paper. List all the living and non-living things you see in the picture.

WANTED: DEAD OR ALIVE

All living things change their size and shape, need food and air, and reproduce themselves.

1. Compare our growth.

_____

_____

2. Compare our food intake.

_____

_____

3. Compare our oxygen (air) intake.

_____

_____

_____

4. Compare the way our babies are born.

_____

_____

5. Compare the way we move.

_____

_____

Compare yourself to one other living thing. Write about your differences and similarities.

Quantitative

Centers

Notes.

Ding A Ling

PURPOSE:

> After completing this center, the student should be able to tell time.

MATERIALS:
Illustration and title
Activity sheets
Directions for making clock
Model clock
Paper plates
Brass fasteners
Tagboard strips
Crayons
Writing paper
Scissors

PROCEDURE:

1. Make model clock and directions chart. Place all materials in the center.

2. Introduce the center to enable the student to select and complete activities in keeping with his own needs.

3. Provide time for the evaluation of each completed activity and record individual progress.

4. Make provision for filing or displaying completed activities.

DING-A-LING

Directions Chart:

Take a paper plate, a brass fastener, two tagboard strips, and a crayon, and make the following:

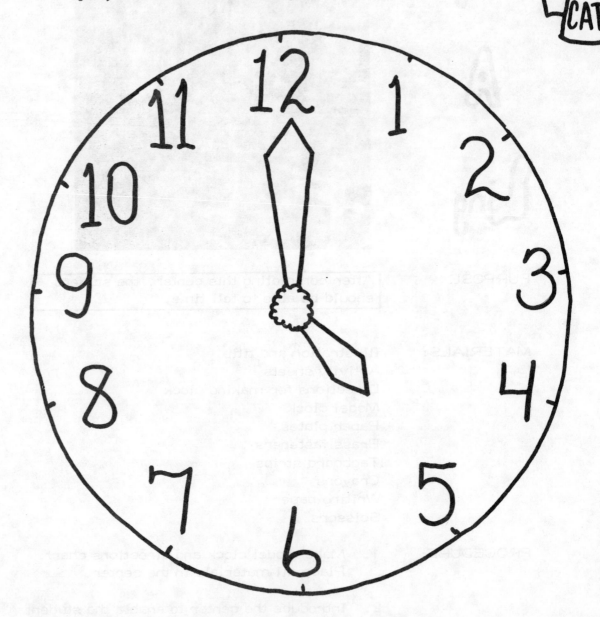

1.   Using your crayon, number the clock face.

2.   Use your tagboard strips to cut hands. Remember to cut the hour hand shorter than the minute hand.

3.   Fasten the two hands to the center of the plate with the brass fastener.

DING-A-LING

Move the hands on the clock you have just made to show
the time given under each of these clock faces.   Draw
hands on each clock to show the correct time.

8:20   7:30

10:15   11:20   12:30

1:35   2:05   3:50

4:10   9:45

Choose your favorite time of day and draw a picture
showing what you like to do at that time.

DING-A-LING

People often use different expressions for the same time. Example: 5:45 – quarter 'til six, and fifteen minutes before six

Write another way to express:

8:15 _____

10:30 _____

7:45 _____

1:20 _____

3:35 _____

5:50 _____

12:20 _____

9:10 _____

2:05 _____

4:40 _____

6:25 _____

11:55 _____

12:00 evening _____

12:00 daytime _____

Write the time you get up, begin school, eat lunch, and go to bed two different ways.

DING-A-LING

Use the clock you made to help you with this sheet.

How many minutes will have passed from:

1:15 to 2:20 _____

6:05 to 7:30 _____

9:20 to 10:50 _____

7:10 to 8:30 _____

10:00 to 10:15 _____

8:05 to 8:40 _____

5:00 to 7:15 _____

4:15 to 4:45 _____

3:35 to 4:35 _____

11:26 to 11:58 _____

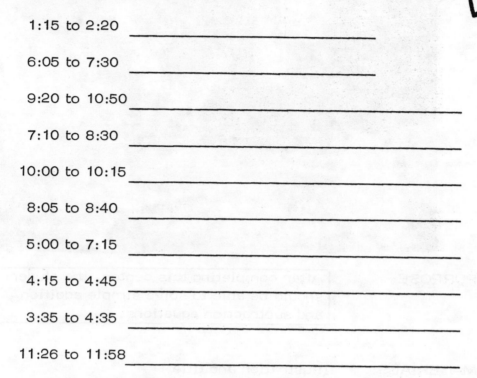

Write the times and the number of minutes it takes for three important things you do every day.

282

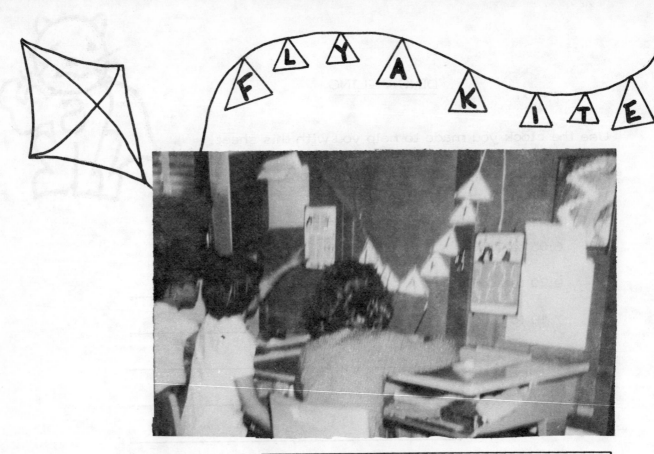

FLY A KITE

PURPOSE: After completing this center, the student
             should be able to solve simple addition
             and subtraction equations.

MATERIALS: Illustration and title
             Activity sheets
             Tagboard
             Crayons
             Pencils

PROCEDURE: 1. Place all materials in the center, including
                 game made according to directions given
                 in "Smarty Cat" activity.

             2. Introduce the center to enable the student
                 to complete activities independently.

             3. Provide time for evaluation of each completed
                 activity and record individual student progress.

             4. Make provision for filing or displaying
                 completed activities.

FLY A KITE

Color this picture:

If the answer is 4 color those spaces red.
If the answer is 5 color those spaces green.
If the answer is 6 color those spaces orange.
If the answer is 7 color those spaces yellow.
If the answer is 8 color those spaces purple.
If the answer is 9 color those spaces blue.

FLY A KITE

$3 + 5 = \boxed{8}$ $9 + 6 = \square$

$7 + 5 = \square$ $6 + 4 = \square$

$8 + 6 = \square$ $7 + 2 = \square$

$3 + 4 = \square$ $8 + 9 = \square$

$5 + 9 = \square$ $5 + 6 = \square$

Draw a story picture for each equation. Color the picture.

Example: $2 + 3 = \boxed{5}$

285

FLY A KITE

Put addition and subtraction facts on pieces of tagboard.
Two players take six cards each and put the remaining
cards in a stack in the middle.

One player will ask for a certain number (i.e. 5). The
other player can either give him 5 or 3 + 2 or 4 + 1, etc.
This will make a book. The player making a book gets
another turn. If the player does not give him a card, he
may draw a card from the stack in the middle. The person
with the most books and out of cards first wins.

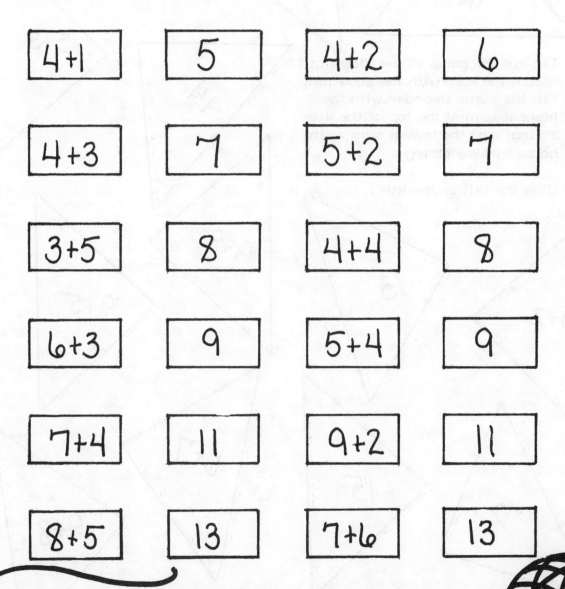

4+1	5	4+2	6
4+3	7	5+2	7
3+5	8	4+4	8
6+3	9	5+4	9
7+4	11	9+2	11
8+5	13	7+6	13

Choose five cards from the deck of cards that have only one
number on them. Write a subtraction equation using this
number as the answer. Example: 5   8 – 3 = 5

FLY A KITE

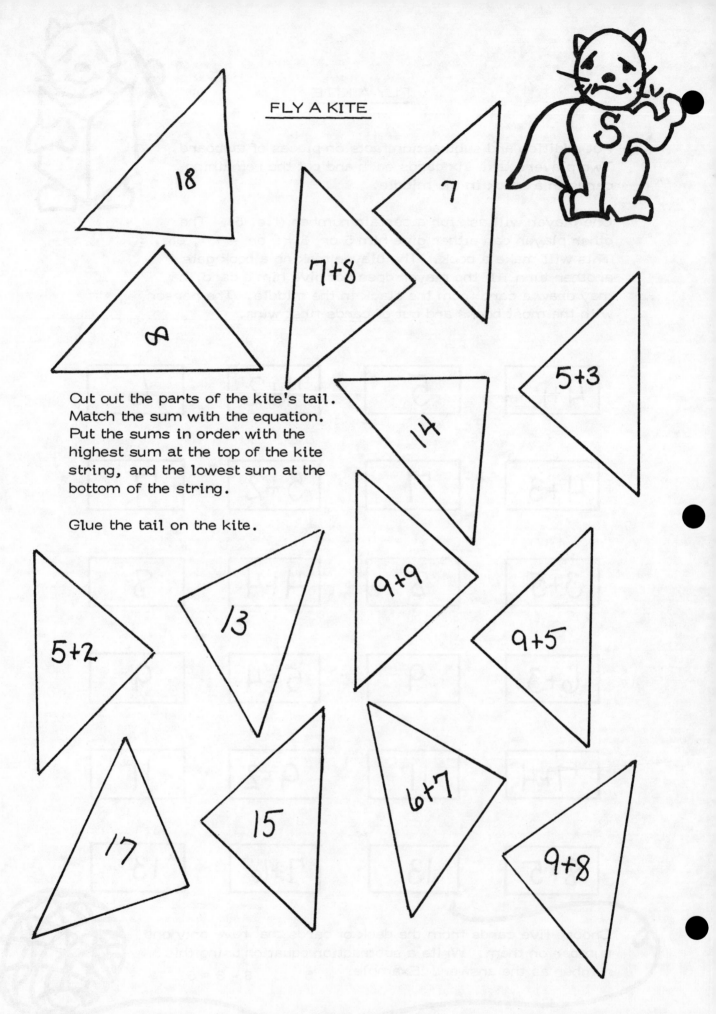

Cut out the parts of the kite's tail.
Match the sum with the equation.
Put the sums in order with the
highest sum at the top of the kite
string, and the lowest sum at the
bottom of the string.

Glue the tail on the kite.

18

7+8

7

8

14

5+3

5+2

13

9+9

9+5

17

15

6+7

9+8

FLY A KITE

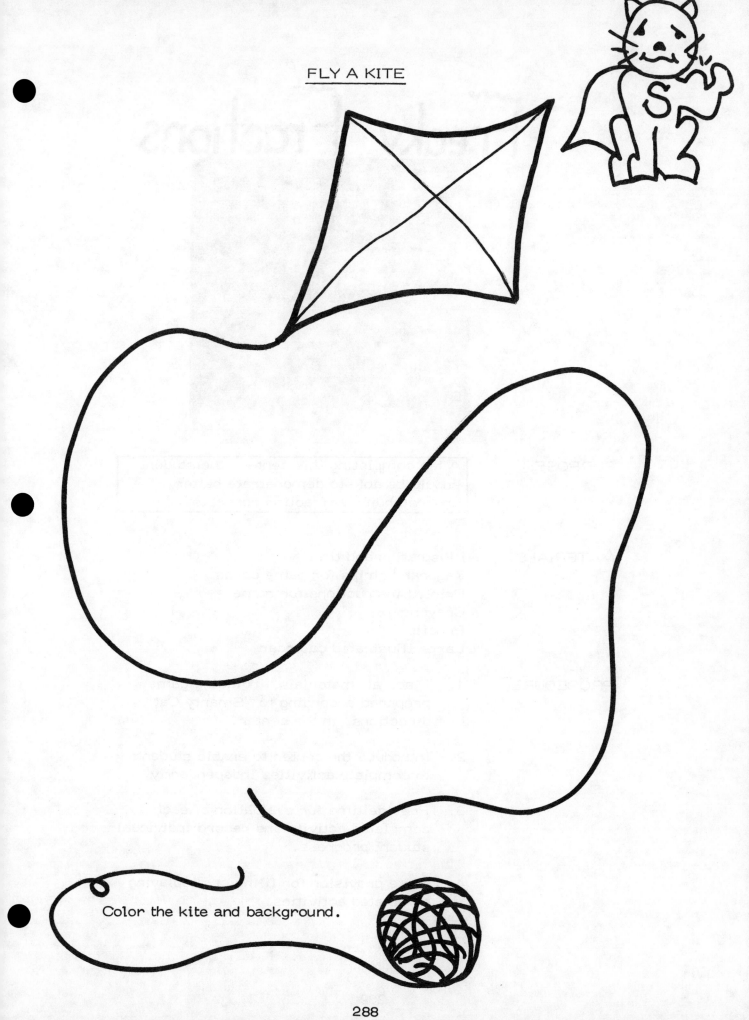

Color the kite and background.

Freaky Fractions

PURPOSE:

> After completing this center, the student should be able to demonstrate better understanding of fraction concepts.

MATERIALS:

Illustration and title
Tagboard strips for game cards
Printed instructions for game
Crayons
Pencils
Large illustrated calendar

PROCEDURE:

1. Place all materials, including game prepared according to "Smarty Cat" directions, in the center.

2. Introduce the center to enable students to complete activities independently.

3. Provide time for evaluation of each completed activity and record individual student progress.

4. Make provision for filing or displaying completed activities.

FREAKY FRACTIONS

Directions:

Color the parts or objects to illustrate the fractions.

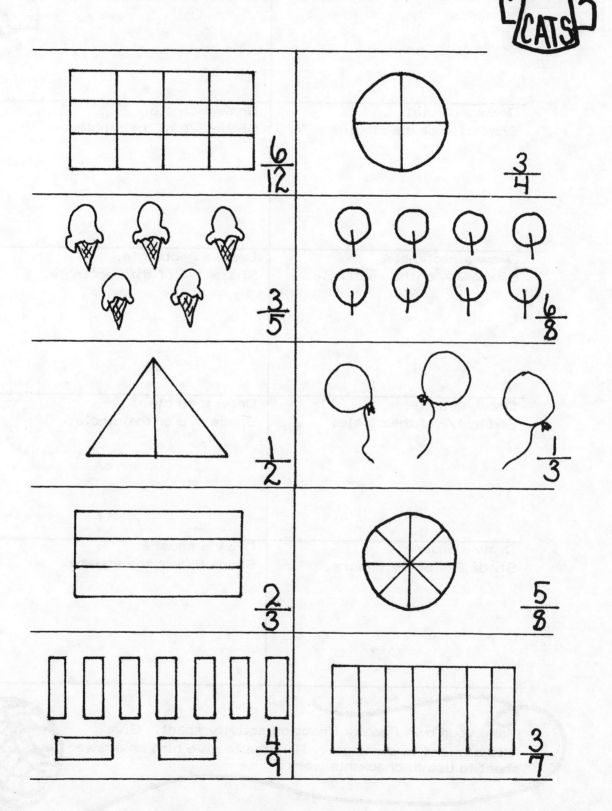

FREAKY FRACTIONS

Draw a square. Shade 1/4 of the square.	Draw a square. Shade 4/8 of the square.
Draw a circle. Shade 1/3 of the circle.	Draw a circle. Shade 3/6 of the circle.
Draw a rectangle. Shade 2/4 of the rectangle.	Draw a rectangle. Shade 1/7 of the rectangle.
Draw a circle. Shade 1/2 of the circle.	Draw a circle. Shade 5/8 of the circle.
Draw a square. Shade 3/4 of the square.	Draw a square. Shade 6/8 of the square.

Make your own Freaky Fraction activity sheet. Give it to a friend to complete. Be sure to give him an answer sheet to use to check his work.

FREAKY FRACTIONS

Directions for Freaky Fraction game:

Play this game as you would play dominos.

1. Each player draws six cards.

2. One card is put down. The other players match
   an end with the equivalent fractions.

   Example:  | 1/4 | 2/8 |

3. As cards are used other cards are drawn until all cards
   have been used.

4. The first player to use all his cards is the winner.

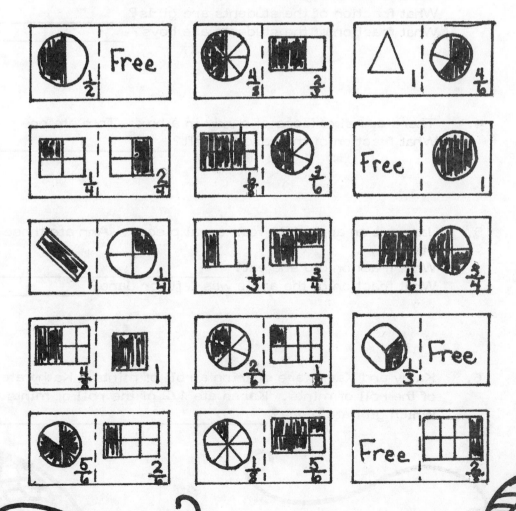

Tell three ways you have used fractions.

FREAKY FRACTIONS

1. Aunt Mary cut a pie in half.
   Then she cut each half in half.
   Write a fraction for each piece. _____

2. Rex cut an orange into two equal pieces.
   What fraction of the orange was each piece? _____

3. Seven students are reading in the library. Four are girls
   and three are boys.
   What fraction of the students are girls? _____
   What fraction of the students are boys? _____

4. There are six pieces of candy in a box. Tom ate one piece.
   What fraction of the candy is left? _____

5. Jane cut an apple into four equal pieces. Ann ate three of the
   pieces.
   What fraction did she eat? _____
   What fraction of the apple was left for Jane? _____

6. Kathy and Karen are sharing a roll of mints. Kathy ate 2/6
   of the roll of mints. Karen ate 1/2 of the roll of mints.
   Which girl ate more? _____

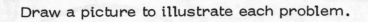

Draw a picture to illustrate each problem.

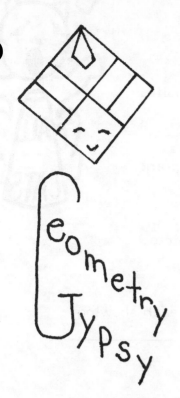

Geometry Gypsy

PURPOSE:

After completing the center, the student should be able to identify geometric figures.

MATERIALS:

Illustration and title
2 blocks of wood 6" x 6"
Tacks
Rubber bands
Magazines
Magic markers or crayons

PROCEDURE:

1. Place all materials in center. Make two geoboards using two blocks of wood 6" x 6" x 1/2". Nail tacks horizontally and vertically on the board so they are equidistant. Nail the tacks halfway in the block of wood. Make different geometric shapes on the geoboard by hooking rubber bands on the tacks. Write the words as given on the "Super Cat" activity sheet on strips of tagboard to make a deck of cards.

2. Introduce the center to enable the student to complete activities independently.

3. Provide time for evaluation of each completed activity and record individual student progress.

4. Make provision for filing or displaying completed activities.

GEOMETRY GYPSY

A part of a line is a ray. A <u>ray</u> has only one end point.

An <u>angle</u> is formed by two rays with the same end point.

A <u>line segment</u> is part of a line and has two end points.

Look around the classroom and draw two pictures each showing
a ray, an angle, and a line segment.

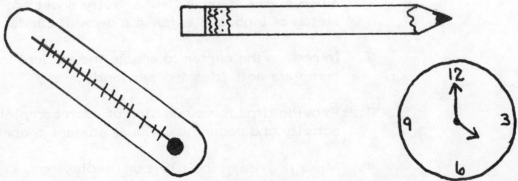

GEOMETRY GYPSY

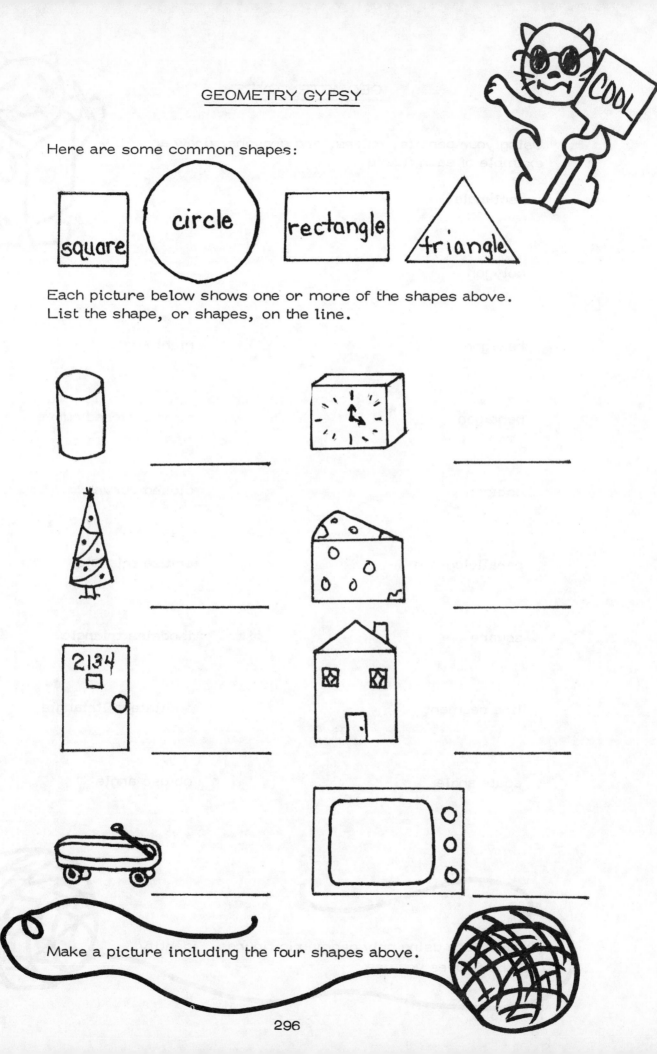

Here are some common shapes:

square   circle   rectangle   triangle

Each picture below shows one or more of the shapes above.
List the shape, or shapes, on the line.

_____   _____

_____   _____

2134

_____   _____

_____   _____

Make a picture including the four shapes above.

GEOMETRY GYPSY

Using your pencils, rulers, and crayons, draw an
example of each figure.

rectangle

polygon

hexagon   right angle

pentagon   simple closed curve

octagon   closed curve

parallelogram   obtuse triangle

square   isoceles triangle

line segment   equilateral triangle

acute angle   obtuse angle

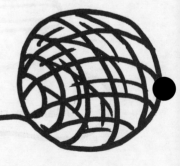

Draw a face using only geometric figures. Identify
all the figures you use.

GEOMETRY GYPSY

From a magazine find pictures that have geometric figures in them. Cut the pictures out. With a black magic marker or black crayon trace around the geometric figure. Paste the pictures on this page to make a geometry collage.

Make a list of all the geometric shapes you used in the collage.

GEOMETRY GYPSY

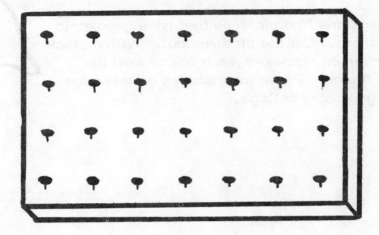

Ideas to put on tagboard strips for deck of cards:

	equilateral		isoceles
rectangle	triangle	polygon	triangle

simple closed	closed	obtuse	
curve	curve	triangle	square

| parallelogram | pentagon | hexagon | octagon |

line segment

Play a challenge game with a friend using geoboards and rubberbands.

1. Shuffle the cards and put them face down.

2. Turn up a card and use a rubberband to make the
    figure given on the card.

3. The first to complete the figure correctly gets a point.

4. Keep score.

5. When all the cards have been used, total the scores and
    find the winner.

Graph ᵗʰᵉ Giraffe

PURPOSE: After completing this center, the student
             should be able to locate information on a
             graph and construct a graph.

MATERIALS: Illustration and title
             Pencils, crayons
             Box of colored cubes or bottle caps
             Activity sheets

PROCEDURE: 1. Prepare directions for game and making
                 graph as explained in "Super Cat" and
                 "Calling All Cats" activities.

             2. Place all materials in the center.

             3. Introduce the center to enable the student
                 to complete activities independently.

             4. Provide time for evaluation of each
                 completed activity and record individual
                 student progress.

             5. Make provision for filing or displaying
                 completed activities.

GRAPH THE GIRAFFE

Use this graph to help you become an artist.

Follow one block at a time and copy the same lines in just one block; then do another. After you complete one row, do another.

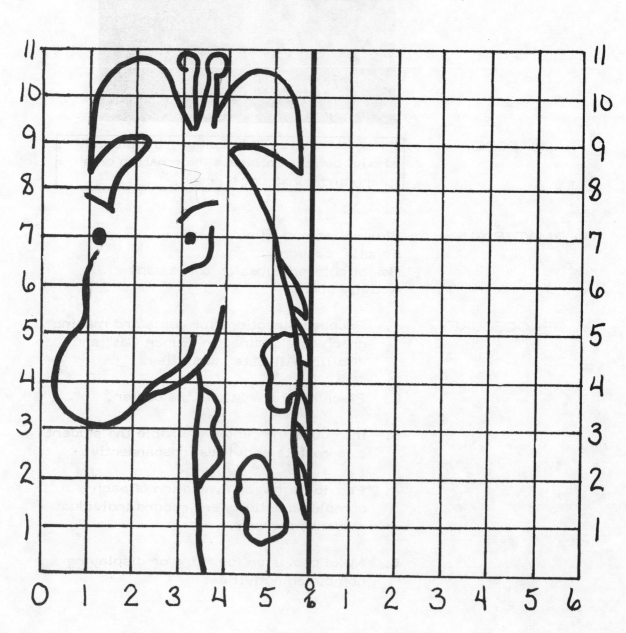

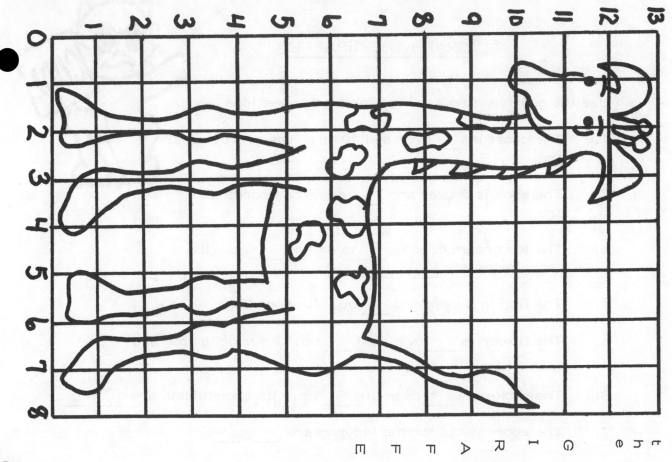

GRAPH

t h e
E F F A R G
I G

GRAPH THE GIRAFFE

Use the graph to find answers for these questions.

1. The ghost is ___ over and 10 up. The coordinates are ___,___.

2. The shoe is 5 over and ___ up. The coordinates are ___,___.

3. The ice cream cone is ___ over and ___ up. Its coordinates are ___,___.

4. The fish is 6 over and ___ up. Its coordinates are ___,___.

5. The flower is ___ over and ___ up. Its coordinates are ___,___.

6. The sucker is ___ over and ___ up. Its coordinates are ___,___.

7. The coordinates for the ladybug are ___, ___.

8. The coordinates for the owl are ___, ___.

9. The coordinates for the tree are ___, ___.

10. What is 5 over and 10 up? _____

11. What is 6 over and 3 up? _____

12. What do you find at (4,3)? _____

13. What do you find at (9,9)? _____

14. What do you find at (10,3)? _____

15. Coordinates (2,6) locate _____.

16. Coordinates (7,4) locate _____.

Choose three objects to locate on the chart. Locate them at these coordinates – (9,4), (4,7), (2,5).

303

GRAPH THE GIRAFFE

Center Illustration: May be enlarged and reproduced on tagboard.

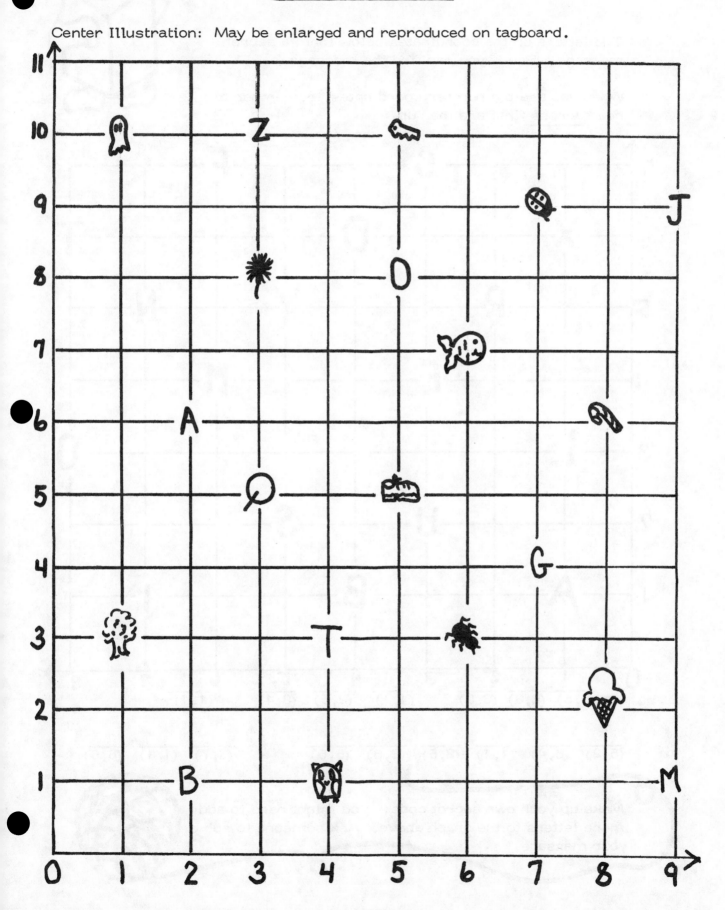

GRAPH THE GIRAFFE

The letters on the coordinates below form a secret message. See if you can find the message.

When you use the number coordinates, remember to read across first and then up.

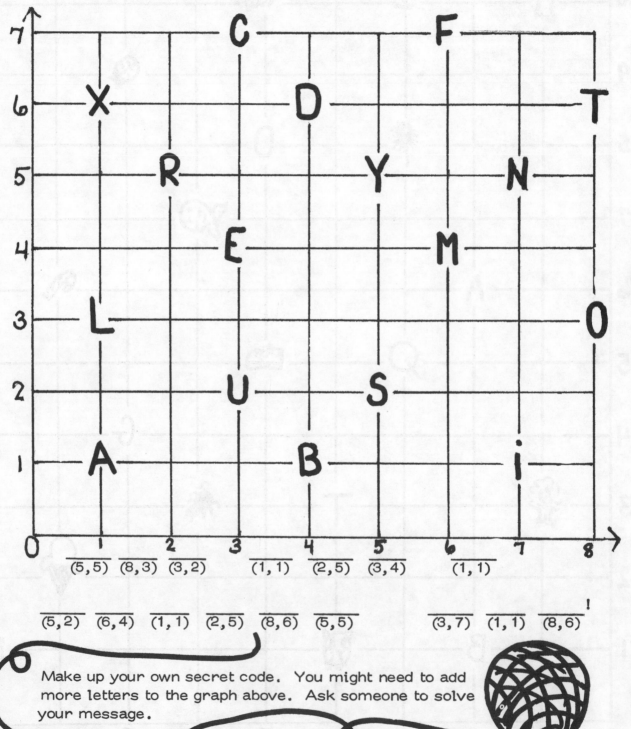

$\overline{(5,5)}$ $\overline{(8,3)}$ $\overline{(3,2)}$ $\overline{(1,1)}$ $\overline{(2,5)}$ $\overline{(3,4)}$ $\overline{(1,1)}$

$\overline{(5,2)}$ $\overline{(6,4)}$ $\overline{(1,1)}$ $\overline{(2,5)}$ $\overline{(8,6)}$ $\overline{(5,5)}$ $\overline{(3,7)}$ $\overline{(1,1)}$ $\overline{(8,6)}$!

Make up your own secret code. You might need to add more letters to the graph above. Ask someone to solve your message.

GRAPH THE GIRAFFE

Using the box with the colored cubes, sort the cubes according to color and make a graph showing the number of cubes for each color.

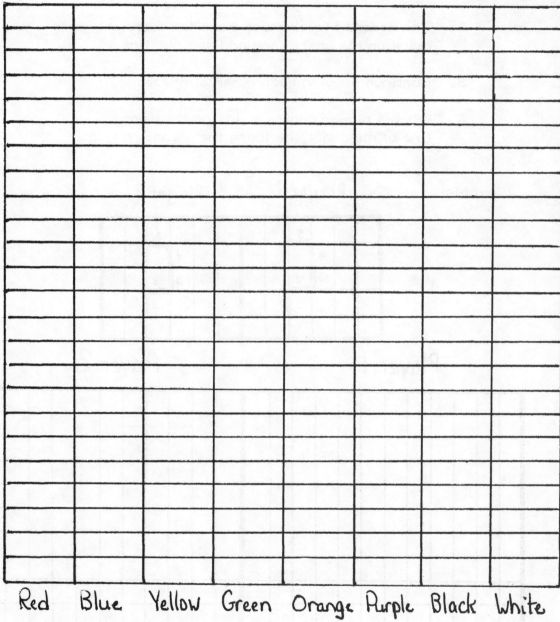

Red   Blue   Yellow   Green   Orange   Purple   Black   White

Take a survey of the class to see what colors are being worn today. Make a graph showing this.

GRAPH THE GIRAFFE

This game is for two players. Use a crayon to mark your lines.

1. The first player marks one line on top of any line on his chart.

2. The second player must make the identical mark on his chart, and add another line.

3. Continue copying each other's moves.

4. When a player copies a line on the wrong line of his chart, he loses the game.

Example:

Player 1   **Player 2**

Player 1   **Player 2**

GRAPH THE GIRAFFE

Take a survey of the boys in the room to find their birthday months. Use the results of the survey to make a graph.

Use a different color crayon for each month.

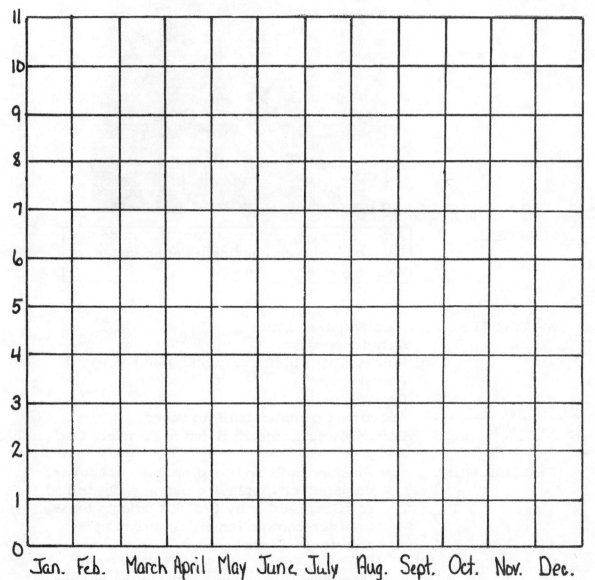

Follow the same directions to make a graph for the girls. Compare the two graphs.

Numberland

PURPOSE: After completing this center, the student
             should be able to develop a better under-
             standing of measurement.

MATERIALS: Illustration and title
             Activity sheets
             Rulers (inch ruler and centimeter ruler)
             Pencils
             Drawing paper
             Apartment complex bulletin board
             Box containing objects listed in "Smarty Cat" activity

PROCEDURE: 1. Prepare bulletin board showing apartment
                 complex for displaying pictures described
                 in "Cool Cat" activity. Put objects to be
                 used for completion of "Smarty Cat"
                 activity in a box.

             2. Introduce the center to enable the student
                 to complete activities independently.

             3. Provide time for evaluation of each completed
                 activity and record individual student progress.

             4. Make provision for filing or displaying
                 completed activities.

NUMBERLAND

12 inches = 1 foot (ft)   3 feet = 1 yard (yd)

Use the ruler and yard stick to compute the following:

_____ inches = 2 feet

_____ feet = 36 inches

_____ inches = 1 foot 6 inches

_____ feet = 1 yard 2 feet

_____ inches = 2 feet 7 inches

_____ yards = 9 feet

_____ yards = 1 yard 3 feet

Complete the following:

1.   16 inches = _____ foot _____ inches
2.   28 inches = _____ feet _____ inches
3.   96 inches = _____ yards _____ feet
4.   54 inches = _____ feet _____ inches
5.   120 inches = _____ yards _____ feet
6.   7 feet 3 inches = _____ yards _____ feet _____ inches
7.   100 inches = _____ feet _____ inches
8.   39 inches = _____ feet _____ inches
9.   2 yards 3 feet = _____ inches
10. 1 yard 9 feet = _____ inches

Add and change the answer to the largest measure.

```
      1 ft.  2 in.                    3 ft. 4 in.
+     1 ft. 10 in.             +      2 ft. 9 in.
  _____  = _____        _____  = _____


      4 ft. 7 in.                    6 ft.  3 in.
+     5 ft. 9 in.             +      3 ft. 12 in.
  _____  = _____        _____  = _____
```

NUMBERLAND

Design your own town house. Your town house has been zoned to meet certain specifications for the apartment complex. Use your ruler to make the correct measurements. To design your town house on a piece of drawing paper follow these directions:

1. The height of the town house, including the roof, is 10 inches. The roof can be any shape.

2. The width of the town house is 8 inches.

3. There are four windows. Each window is 1-3/4 inches wide and 2 inches tall.

4. The one door is 2-1/2 inches tall and 2 inches wide.

5. Make shutters on the downstairs windows 1/2 inch wide and 2 inches tall.

6. Put flower boxes under the windows upstairs. Make them 1/2 inch tall and 1-3/4 inches wide.

7. Place a doorknob one inch from the bottom of the door.

8. Add a chimney one inch wide and as tall as you wish.

9. Add drapes to your windows if you like.

10. Color your town house and cut it out. Add it to the apartment complex on the bulletin board.

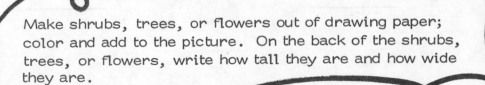

Make shrubs, trees, or flowers out of drawing paper; color and add to the picture. On the back of the shrubs, trees, or flowers, write how tall they are and how wide they are.

NUMBERLAND

Using an inch ruler, measure the objects in the "Smarty Cat" box. Make a graph and color it to show how many inches long each object is.

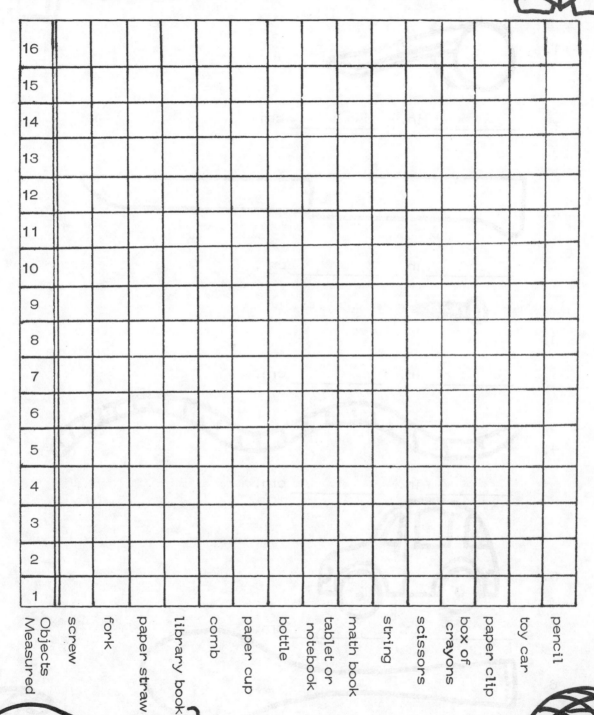

Use a centimeter ruler and measure the same objects. Make a graph and color it. Compare the number of inches and centimeters each object has.

NUMBERLAND

In many countries centimeter rulers are used. Use an inch ruler and a centimeter ruler to compare the measurements of these objects.

1.

_____ in. _____ cm.

2.

_____ in _____ cm.

3.

_____ in. _____ cm.

4.

_____ in. _____ cm.

5.

_____ in. _____ cm.

6.

_____ in. _____ cm.

Write a sentence explaining the difference between an inch and a centimeter.

  # Piggy Bank

PURPOSE: | After completing this center, the student should be able to solve problems involving simple monetary concepts.

MATERIALS: Illustration and title
Crayons
Activity sheets

PROCEDURE:
1. Place all materials in the center.

2. Verbally introduce the center to enable the student to complete activities independently.

3. Provide time for evaluation of each completed activity and record individual student progress.

4. Make provision for filing or displaying completed activities.

314

PIGGY BANK

Write the value in dollars and cents.

1. one dollar and thirty-one cents _____

2. four dollars and fifteen cents _____

3. six dollars and eighty-seven cents _____

4. nine dollars and sixty-nine cents _____

5. five hundred thirty cents _____

Circle the greater amount.

1.	415¢	$4.25	6.	637¢		$6.40
2.	150¢	$1.46	7.	$1.89		180¢
3.	$3.64	370¢	8.	$3.36		345¢
4.	$1.25	123¢	9.	152¢		$1.50
5.	732¢	$7.25	10.	470¢		$4.69

If the amount is less than $1.00, write No. If the amount is more than $1.00, write Yes.

1. $1.23 ___   3. $2.36 ___   5. $0.85 ___   7. $1.10 ___

2. $0.90 ___   4. $1.01 ___   6. $0.15 ___   8. $3.18 ___

Coins				Value in
Dollars	Dimes	Nickels	Pennies	Dollars and Cents
4	1	3	5	
6	2		18	
3	3	4	16	
8	8	2	3	

PIGGY BANK

Write an equation showing each problem.

1. Three ice cream cones cost 24¢.
    How much does one ice cream cone cost?

    _____

2. Milk costs 32¢ per quart.
    Four quarts = one gallon
    How much will one gallon of milk cost?

    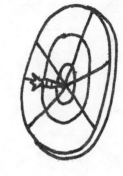

    _____

3. A dart game cost $1.29. A model cost $0.98.
    How much more does the dart game cost than
    the model?

    _____

4. Daddy mailed a package. He had to put two 8¢ stamps and
    one 11¢ stamp on the package before he mailed it. How
    much did the stamps cost?

    _____

5. Which cost more, eight 5¢ candy bars or nine 6¢ lollipops?

    _____

6. Tommy went to the fair. He spent $1.20 on rides. Each ride
    was 10¢. How many rides did he have?

    _____

7. Mary bought four rulers for 36¢. How much was each ruler?

    _____

8. Ann took two friends to the movie. She had 50¢. She bought
    herself and each friend a bag of popcorn. Each bag of popcorn
    cost 16¢. How much money did she have left?

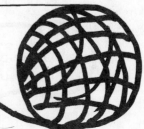

Write two story problems using the amounts of money
given.

    1.   76¢ and 52¢
    2.   4¢ and 24¢

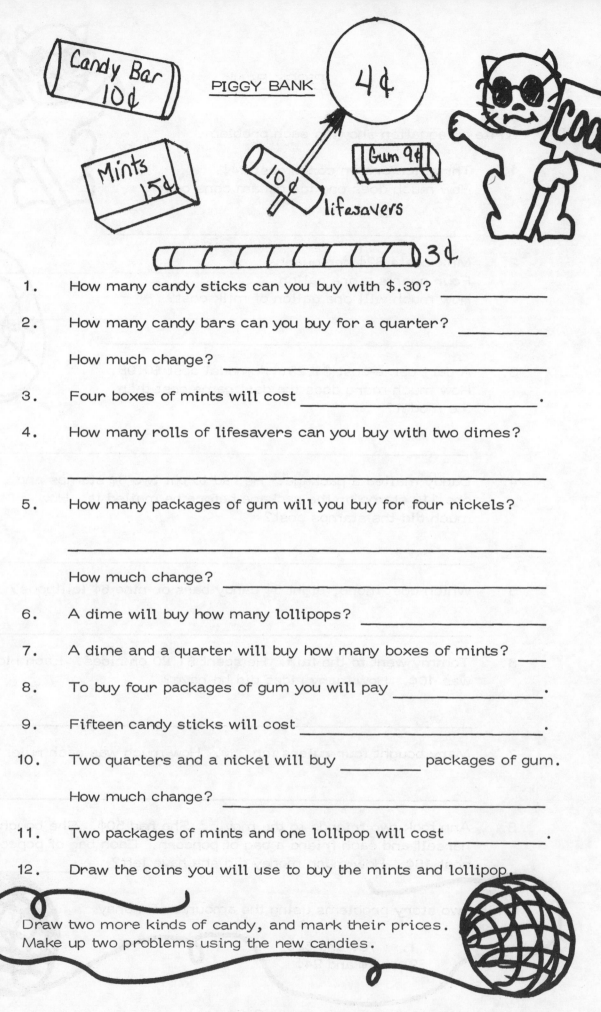

Candy Bar 10¢

PIGGY BANK

4¢

Mints 15¢

10¢ lifesavers

Gum 9¢

COOL

3¢

1. How many candy sticks can you buy with $.30? _____

2. How many candy bars can you buy for a quarter? _____

How much change? _____

3. Four boxes of mints will cost _____.

4. How many rolls of lifesavers can you buy with two dimes?

_____

5. How many packages of gum will you buy for four nickels?

_____

How much change? _____

6. A dime will buy how many lollipops? _____

7. A dime and a quarter will buy how many boxes of mints? __

8. To buy four packages of gum you will pay _____.

9. Fifteen candy sticks will cost _____.

10. Two quarters and a nickel will buy _____ packages of gum.

How much change? _____

11. Two packages of mints and one lollipop will cost _____.

12. Draw the coins you will use to buy the mints and lollipop.

Draw two more kinds of candy, and mark their prices.
Make up two problems using the new candies.

PIGGY BANK

Fill in the squares by supplying the correct answers.

Cost of 1	2	3	4
Q 2¢			
1¢			
8¢			

Cost of 1	5	6
5¢		
10¢		
15¢		

Cost of 2	4	6	8
2 for 8¢			
2 for 10¢			
2 for 5¢			

Cost of 3	6	9	12
3 for 25¢			
3 for 10¢			
3 for 12¢			

Cost of 10	20	25
10 for 40¢		

Cost of 25	50	75
25 for 5¢		

How much would five apples cost? _____ How much would one banana be? _____ Fifty lollipops for your class would cost _____ . Six doughnuts would cost _____ . How much would it cost to buy ice cream bars for everyone in your family?

318

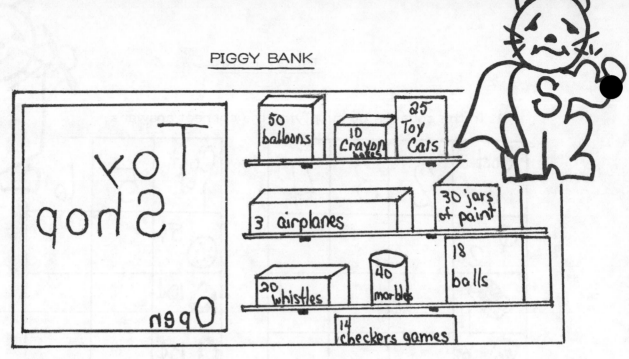

Figure out the cost of each toy!

1.   The balloon box cost $2.00. One balloon will be _____ .

2.   The three airplanes cost $2.10. How much will one be?

_____ .

3.   Forty marbles cost $.80. One will cost _____ .

4.   The whistles in the box cost $4.20. One will cost _____ .

5.   Thirty jars of paint cost $3.60. One jar is _____ .

1.   If you wished to buy two toy cars, you would pay _____ .

2.   Twenty marbles would cost _____ .

3.   Forty balloons for a party will cost _____ .

4.   Five jars of paint will cost _____ .

5.   Three balls will cost _____ .

Add another box of toys to the shelf. Compute the cost of the entire box, and of each toy.

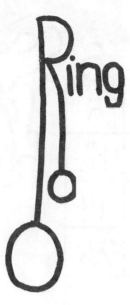 # Ring My Chimes

PURPOSE: After completing this center, the student
               should be able to demonstrate better
               understanding of time.

MATERIALS: Illustration and title
               Activity sheets
               Resource books
               Drawing paper
               Crayons

PROCEDURE: 1.   Place all materials in the center.

               2.   Involve students in a group discussion
                    of the calendar. Explain center activities
                    to enable students to complete them
                    independently at their own rate.

               3.   Provide time for evaluation of each
                    completed activity and record individual
                    student progress.

               4.   Make provision for filing or displaying
                    completed activities.

CALLING
CALL
CATS

S	M	T	W	Th	F	S
		1	2	3	4	5
6	7	8	9	10	11	12
13	14	15	16	17	18	19
20	21	22	23	24	25	26
27	28	29	30	31		

1. How many days are in a week? _____

2. How many months are in a year? _____

3. What will the date be a week from the 2nd? _____

4. List the dates of all the Mondays on the calendar above.

    _____ _____ _____ _____

5. How many days are there between the 11th and the 25th?

    _____ How many weeks is this? _____

6. On the 30th, what was the date two weeks ago? _____

7. On the 26th how many Fridays will be left in the month?

    _____

8. On the 14th how many Sundays will be left in the month?

    _____

9. What day of the week will the first day of the following month
    fall on? _____

RING MY CHIMES

Use an encyclopedia to help you complete the following.
Make your sentences interestingly creative.

A calendar is __ _____

_____

The Gregorian calendar is _____

_____

_____

_____

The Hebrew calendar is _____

_____

_____

_____

The Islamic calendar is _____

_____

_____

_____

_____

Design a Gregorian calendar.

RING MY CHIMES

Imagine a world without time. Write about the kind of life you would be living in a world without clocks, hours, minutes, weeks or years.

_____

_____

_____

_____

_____

_____

_____

A time capsule is to be made. It will contain important items to inform people thousands of years from now about our civilization. Write a paragraph or a story telling what you think should be put in the time capsule.

_____

_____

_____

_____

_____

_____

_____

Design the capsule. Tell what materials the capsule will be made from, and where it should be placed to be found.

RING MY CHIMES

Use a resource book to help you answer some of these questions.

1. We use clocks because _____

    _____

2. The measurement units on a clock are _____

    and _____

3. There are _____ minutes in an hour.

4. There are _____ hours in a day.

Clocks were used thousands of years ago.

5. The water clock was _____

    _____

6. Find two other kinds of devices that were once used to tell time. Explain how they worked.

    (a) _____

    _____

    _____

    (b) _____

    _____

    _____

7. One of the newest clocks we have is an atomic clock. Gather information to help you explain it.

    _____

    _____

8. List all the means of telling time you use.

    _____ _____ _____

Draw and label four ways to tell time.

$hopping $pree

PURPOSE: After completing this center the student should be able to add dollars and cents.

MATERIALS: Illustration and title
Gift catalogs
Newspaper food ads
Pencils
Activity sheets
Crayons
Drawing paper

PROCEDURE:

1. Place the illustration, title, activity sheets, newspapers and catalogs in the center.

2. Introduce the center to enable the student to select and complete the activities in keeping with his own needs.

3. Provide time for the evaluation of each completed activity and record individual progress.

4. Make provision for filing or displaying completed activities.

SHOPPING SPREE

Christmas and Hanukkah are almost here. What gifts
would you like to get? Look in the gift catalogue and
select ten gifts you would like to receive. When you
finish shopping add the amount of money all the gifts
would cost.

Gift	Cost of Gift
	Total

SHOPPING SPREE

Have you decided what holiday gifts you will give your family and friends? Select gifts for them from the gift catalog. When you have finished shopping, add the amount of money all your gifts will cost.

Person Receiving Gift	Gift	Cost of Gift
		Total

Tell how you will earn the money, and how long it will take. Draw yourself earning the money.

SHOPPING SPREE

Newspapers help shoppers be aware of special sales and reduced prices. See how much you will need to spend to buy the items listed below.

1.   9-1b. turkey will cost _____
          Turkeys are 65¢ per pound.

2.   3 pounds of cranberries will cost _____
          Cranberries are 49¢ per pound.

3.   4 pounds of beans will cost _____
          Beans are 35¢ per pound.

4.   4 pounds of potatoes will cost _____
          A 2-1b. bag of potatoes is $1.16.

5.   2 loaves of bread will cost _____
          Bread is 35¢ a loaf.

6.   4 pounds of pears and apples will cost _____
          Apples and pears are 59¢ per pound.

7.   3 gallons of milk will cost _____
          Milk is 61¢ a half-gallon.

8.   3 pumpkin pies will cost _____
          It costs 85¢ to make one pumpkin pie.

Total the cost of this meal and see how much you will need to spend.

328

SHOPPING SPREE

Choose from the newspaper ads what you plan to
serve for your holiday dinner.

	Your choice	Cost per pound	Total Cost
1. Meat			
2. Vegetable			
3. Vegetable			
4. Vegetable			
5. Fruit			
6. Fruit			
7. Salad			
8. Salad			
9. Beverage			
10. Beverage			
11. Dessert			
12. Dessert			
13. Candy			
14. Nuts			

Total the cost of the dinner.........................$

Choose three more foods you would like for your
holiday dinner. Draw pictures of them and give their
cost.

Snack Shop

PURPOSE:

After completing this center, the student should be able to understand and use liquid and dry measurements.

MATERIALS:

Illustration and title
Cup measure
Pint, quart, half-gallon and gallon jars
Measuring spoons
Water
Dictionary
Shelf for bulletin board
Drawing paper
Crayons
Activity sheets

PROCEDURE:

1. Place all materials in the center. Arrange the bulletin board and shelf.

2. Introduce the center to enable the student to complete the activities independently.

3. Provide time for evaluation of each completed activity and record individual progress.

4. Make provision for filing or displaying completed activities.

SNACK SHOP

Using the measuring utensils and water, compute the following:

_____ teaspoons = 1 tablespoon

_____ tablespoons = 1 cup

_____ cups = 1 pint

_____ pints = 1 quart

_____ quarts = 1 gallon

_____ ounces = 1 cup

_____ ounces = 1 pound

_____ = 1 dozen

Use the chart you just completed or measure to find the following answers:

4 cups = _____ pints

1 quart – _____ ounces

24 = _____ dozen

1 pint = _____ tablespoon

1 quart and 2 cups = _____ pints

2 gallons = _____ quarts

3 cups = _____ ounces

15 teaspoons = _____ tablespoons

6 pints = _____ cups

2 quarts and 2 pints = _____ pints

Use a dictionary, an encyclopedia, or a math book to find abbreviations for the following words:

pints _____   gallons _____   teaspoons _____
quarts _____   ounces _____   tablespoons _____
                     dozen _____

331

SNACK SHOP

We need a change! For lunch we are going on a picnic.
We have voted on this menu:

Hot dogs and buns	Hawaiian punch
Potato chips	Cookies and ice cream

This food is packaged:

    12 hot dogs per pound
    12 buns per package
    36 oz. potato chips per package
    32 oz. punch per can
    1 dozen cookies per package
    1/2 gallon ice cream per carton

There are 24 students going on the picnic.

Each student will eat:	We need to buy for the picnic:
1 hot dog	_____ pounds of hot dogs
1 hot dog bun	_____ packages of buns
6 oz. potato chips	_____ bags of chips
8 oz. punch	_____ cans of punch
4 cookies	_____ dozen cookies
8 oz. ice cream	_____ 1/2 gallon cartons ice cream

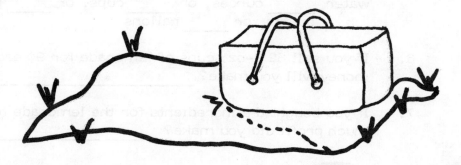

Each student has decided to bring a friend. How many will
be going on the picnic now? Look at your chart and compute
the amount of food you need to buy now.

SNACK SHOP

It's summertime and you need some excitement and money! You decide to put up a lemonade stand. Before you are able to open for business you must get your supplies together. Follow the directions to find how successful you will be as a business person. Good luck!

Recipe for Lemonade

Juice from 1/2 lemon
2 teaspoons sugar
8 ounces water

Squeeze lemon in glass. Add sugar and water. Stir.

1. How many cups of lemonade will you be able to sell if you follow the lemonade recipe as it is given? _____

2. How many cups of lemonade do you plan to sell? _____

3. How much will you charge for each cup of lemonade? _____

4. How much money will you make from all your lemonade sales? _____

5. Business is good on Saturday. You can sell 32 cups of lemonade. Using the recipe, how much of the following will you need:

    lemons _____, or _____ dozen and _____ lemons
    sugar _____ teaspoons, or _____ cups
    water _____ ounces, or _____ cups, or _____ pints, or ____ quarts, or _____ gallons

6. If you sell 32 8–oz. cups of lemonade for 9¢ each, how much money will you make? _____

7. If you bought the ingredients for the lemonade for $1.86, how much profit did you make? _____

Design your lemonade stand. Put yourself in the picture.

SNACK SHOP

You've just opened a snack shop.

```
                    MENU
Ice Cream (all flavors).................15¢ per scoop
Sundaes (chocolate, butterscotch).......40¢
Milk Shakes (vanilla, chocolate,
             strawberry) ..............35¢
Banana Split..........................55¢
Floats................................30¢
```

For the grand opening, you plan to serve 160 people.

Each scoop of ice cream = 4 oz.
Syrup on 1 scoop ice cream = 2 tablespoons
Milk in milk shake = 8 oz.
Soda pop in a float = 8 oz.
4 bananas = 1 pound
1 banana per banana split

No. Sold	Ingredients	Total Amount Served		
50	scoops of ice cream	__oz. or	_____1/2 gal.	
30	double-scoop sundaes	__oz. or	_____ gal.	
	butterscotch syrup for sundaes	__Tblsp. or	_____ cups	
40	milkshakes – 1 scoop ice cream	__oz. ice cream		
	milkshakes – milk	__cups milk	_____qt. milk	
20	banana splits – bananas	__bananas	_____ lbs.	
	banana splits – 3 scoops ice cream	__oz.	_____1/2 gal.	
	banana split syrup	__Tblsp.	_____cups	
20	floats – 1 scoop ice cream	__cups	_____qts.	
	soda pop for floats	__oz.	_____gal.	

Draw what you would order in the snack shop. Cut it out and display it on the shop's shelf.

A Web of Riddles

PURPOSE:	After completing this center, the student should be able to read and write Roman numerals.

MATERIALS:
Illustration and title
Resource book or encyclopedia
Activity sheets
Box for secret codes
Pencils

PROCEDURE:

1. Print the secret code to be used with "Smarty Cat" and "Super Cat" activities on tagboard. The code may be displayed or put in a box.

2. Place all materials in the center.

3. Introduce the center to enable the student to complete activities independently.

4. Provide time for evaluation of each completed activity and record individual student progress.

5. Make provisions for filing or displaying completed activities.

WEB OF RIDDLES

The numerals we use most are Arabic. Roman numerals give us an optional number system.

Use an encyclopedia to find out the value of each Roman numeral.

I = _____   X = _____   C = _____   M = _____

V = _____   L = _____   D = _____

Where were Roman numerals first used? _____

_____

List three ways Roman numerals are used today. _____

_____

_____

Write these Arabic numerals
in Roman numerals:

17	_____
4	_____
29	_____
56	_____
123	_____
519	_____
81	_____
63	_____
1,326	_____
35	_____

Write these Roman numerals
in Arabic numerals:

XII	_____
III	_____
LXXV	_____
CXLI	_____
XXVIII	_____
XXXIX	_____
MCCLVI	_____
DXV	_____
MCMLXXIV	_____
LXXXVIII	_____

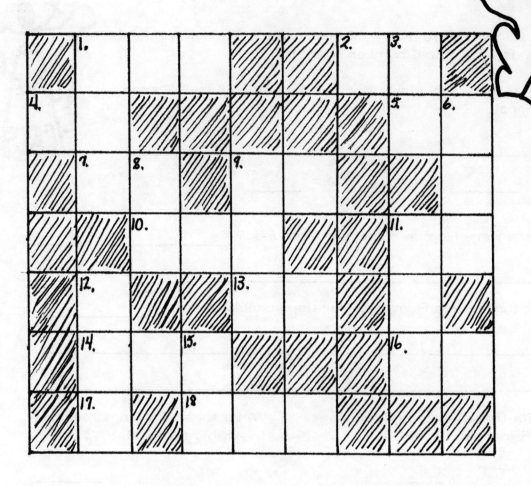

Change these Roman numerals to Arabic numerals to help you
complete the puzzle.

Across:
1. DLXIV
2. LXXXIII
4. XXIII
5. XCII
7. XLIII
9. LI
10. DCCXXII
11. LXIV
13. L
14. CDXXXI
16. XXV
17. VII
18. CXI

Down:
1. DXXXIV
3. XXXIX
6. CCXXIV
8. XXXVII
9. DXXV
11. DCLXXXII
12. DCCXLVII
15. XI

WEB OF RIDDLES

Secret Code:

A = 7 + 3		N = 20 + 20
B = 4 + 5		O = 10 + 9
C = 1 + 2		P = 7 + 4
D = 3 + 4		Q = 9 + 8
E = 5 + 3		R = 9 + 5
F = 16 – 10		S = 41 + 9
G = 18 – 16		T = 2 + 2
H = 10 + 10		U = 200 – 100
I = 1 + 0		V = 10 – 5
J = 100 + 100		W = 8 + 7
K = 8 + 8		X = 20 + 10
L = 2000 – 1000		Y = 8 + 4
M = 6 + 7		Z = 9 + 9

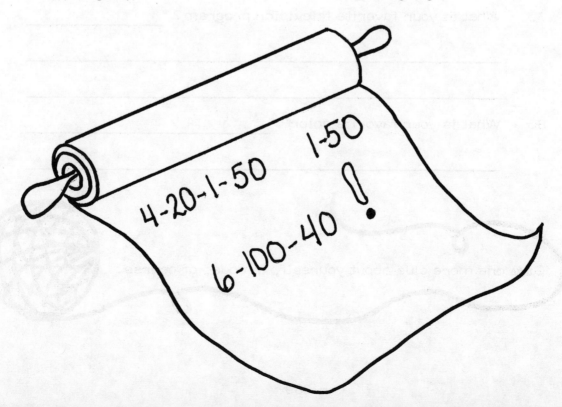

WEB OF RIDDLES

Read the questions below and answer them in Roman numerals. Write your answer by finding the Arabic numeral on the secret code. Then convert the Arabic numeral into a Roman numeral. Put a dash between each Roman numeral.

1.   What is your name? _____

_____

2.   How old are you? _____

3.   Where do you live? _____

_____

4.   What grade are you in? _____

5.   What is your favorite sport? _____

_____

6.   What is your favorite food? _____

_____

7.   What is your favorite television program? _____

_____

_____

8.   What is your favorite color? _____

_____

Give one more clue about yourself, in code, of course.

WEB OF RIDDLES

Use the secret code to figure out the secret message.
The code is in Arabic numerals and you must change them
to Roman numerals to understand the message.

XV – XX – X – IV   VII – I – VII

— — — —   — — —

XIX – XL – VIII   IV – XIX – XL – L – I – M

— — —   — — — — — —

L – X – XII   IV – XIX   IV – XX – VIII

— — —   — —   — — —

XIX – IV – XX – VIII – XIV   IV – XIX – XL – L – I – M?

— — — — —   — — — — — —?

M – VIII – IV – ' L   II – VIII – IV

— — — ' —   — — —

VII – XIV – VIII – L – L – VIII – VII,   IV XX VIII

— — — — — — — —,   — — —

VII – XIX – III – IV – XIX – XIV   I – L

— — — — — —   — —

IV – X – XVI – I – XL – II   C – L   XIX – C – IV

— — — — — —   — —   — — —

IV – XIX – XL – I – II – XX – IV

— — — — — — —

Make up a secret message using Roman numerals and put in
the box for your friends to figure out.

Weighing Away

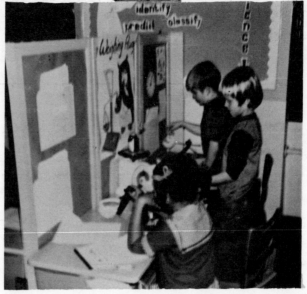

PURPOSE: After completing this center, the student
            should demonstrate competency in using
            a balance scale and a scale that measures
            pounds and ounces.

MATERIALS: Illustration and title
            Balance scale
            Scale measuring ounces and pounds
            Candy for treats
            Objects listed in "Calling All Cats" and
            "Cool Cat" activities

PROCEDURE: 1. Place all materials in center.

            2. Introduce the center to enable the student
                to complete activities independently.

            3. Provide time for evaluation of each completed
                activity and record individual student progress.

            4. Make provisions for filing or displaying
                completed activities.